Charles B. Todd

**A brief history of the city of New York**

Charles B. Todd

**A brief history of the city of New York**

ISBN/EAN: 9783743350328

Manufactured in Europe, USA, Canada, Australia, Japa

Cover: Foto ©ninafisch / pixelio.de

Manufactured and distributed by brebook publishing software (www.brebook.com)

Charles B. Todd

**A brief history of the city of New York**

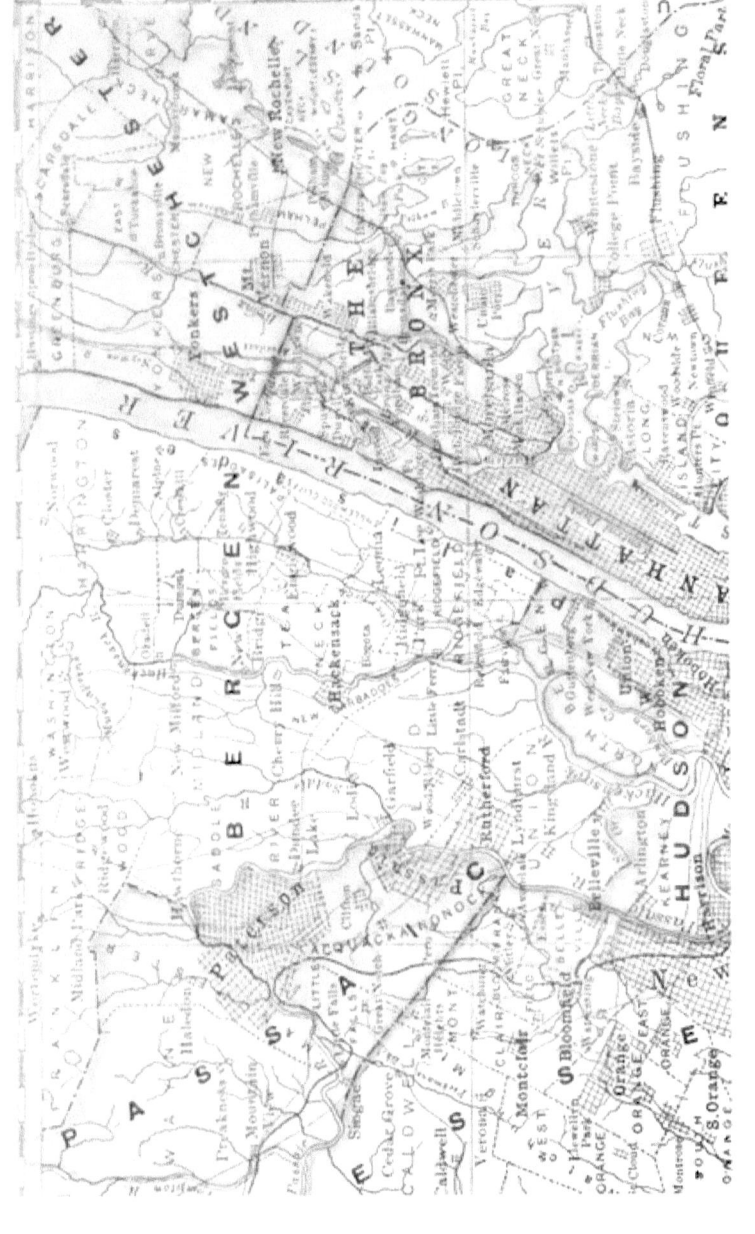

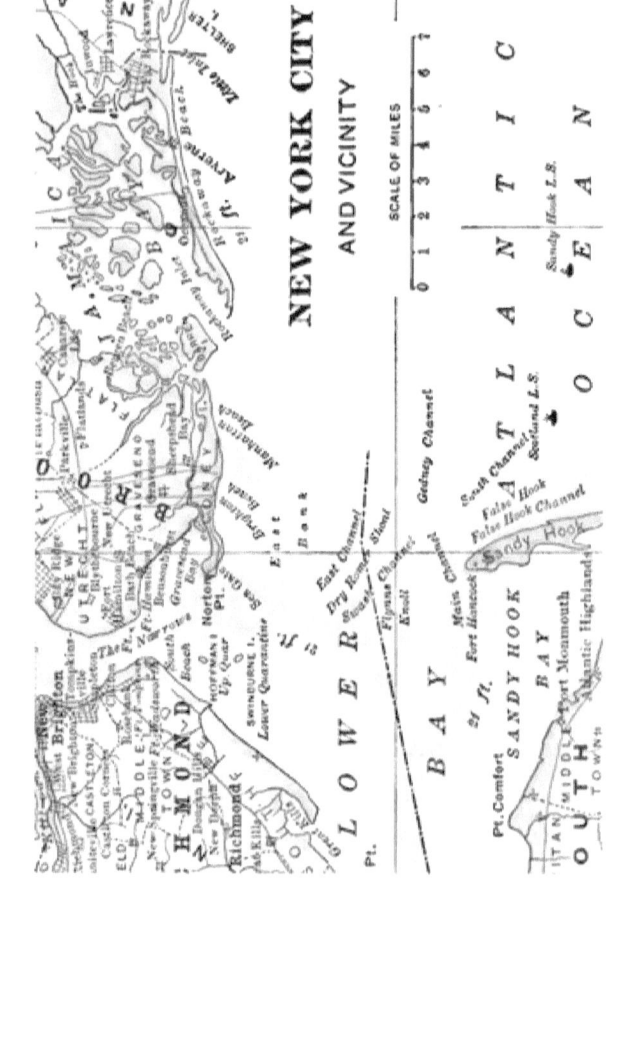

# A BRIEF HISTORY

## OF THE

# CITY OF NEW YORK

BY

CHARLES B. TODD

*Member of the New York Historical Society,
Author of "The Story of the City of New York,"
"The Story of Washington, the National Capital," etc.*

NEW YORK ∴ CINCINNATI ∴ CHICAGO
AMERICAN BOOK COMPANY

# PREFACE.

THIS volume was written at the suggestion of public school teachers and members of the City History Club, as a text-book for use in the public and private schools of New York, as well as for all others interested in the study of the city's striking and romantic history. It has been the author's aim to present this history concisely, accurately, impartially, and at the same time to weave into the narrative such romantic and picturesque incidents, such details of manners, customs, and domestic life, as would lend it local color and render the picture clear and complete. The causes which led to the founding of the city, and the men and the agencies responsible for its wonderful growth, have not been forgotten.

In a work so condensed it was impossible to notice all the events in the city's history. For these the reader is referred to the larger and more elaborate histories of the city by Mary L. Booth, David T. Valentine, Martha J. Lamb, William L. Stone, Benson J. Lossing, the "Memorial History of New York," edited by General James Grant Wilson, and the author's larger work, "The Story of the City of New York." For material the author has drawn on the large store gathered for his "Story of the City of New York," first published in 1888, together with important data collected since that work was issued. His principal sources have been "The Documentary History of the State of New York," the publications of the New York Historical Society, the "Manual of the Corporation," the newspaper files, diaries, scrapbooks, broadsides, and pamphlets contained in the libraries of the New York Historical Society, the New York Public Library, and the library of Columbia College, to all of which he has had free access. Where conflicting accounts of the same event were given, he has chosen that which seemed the more probable. Above all things he has endeavored to write impartially and without bias.

As before stated, the book is intended primarily for the young. Events with us move rapidly. In twenty years, if present conditions continue, New York will surpass London, and the school children of to-day will then hold in their hands the destinies of the greatest city in the world. If they become familiar with the history of their city in youth, they will love it, will take an interest in its affairs, and will be far more likely to guide its destinies aright.

But although it is intended for the young, the author hopes that his little book will appeal to the great mass of citizens who have but little time for reading, and to whom the larger histories are sealed books.

C. B. T.

NEW YORK, September 1, 1899.

# CONTENTS.

|     |     | PAGE |
| --- | --- | --- |
| I. | INTRODUCTORY | 7 |
| II. | THE DUTCH DYNASTY — PETER MINUIT | 14 |
| III. | WOUTER VAN TWILLER | 23 |
| IV. | WILHELM KIEFT | 29 |
| V. | PETRUS STUYVESANT | 35 |
| VI. | DUTCH MANNERS AND CUSTOMS | 52 |
| VII. | THE ENGLISH COLONIAL PERIOD | 75 |
| VIII. | THE ENGLISH COLONIAL PERIOD (*Continued*) — LEISLER'S REVOLT | 83 |
| IX. | THE APPROACH OF THE REVOLUTION | 99 |
| X. | THE PEOPLE UNDER BRITISH RULE | 109 |
| XI. | THROWING OFF THE BRITISH YOKE | 136 |
| XII. | THE BATTLE OF LONG ISLAND | 151 |
| XIII. | THE BATTLE OF HARLEM HEIGHTS | 174 |
| XIV. | NEW YORK IN THE GRASP OF THE INVADER | 186 |
| XV. | NEW YORK THE CAPITAL CITY | 195 |
| XVI. | THE GROWTH OF PARTIES | 203 |
| XVII. | HER RISE TO COMMERCIAL POWER | 214 |
| XVIII. | THE ERIE CANAL | 220 |

|        |                                        |      |
|--------|----------------------------------------|------|
| XIX.   | The Railroad .                         | 228  |
| XX.    | Typical New York Merchants             | 230  |
| XXI.   | Ships and Sailors                      | 240  |
| XXII.  | New York in the Civil War              | 250  |
| XXIII. | An Old Man's Recollections of New York | 259  |
| XXIV.  | A Hundred Years of Progress            | 272  |
| XXV.   | Greater New York                       | 278  |
| XXVI.  | Brooklyn                               | 287  |
| XXVII. | The Bronx                              | 290  |
|        | Index                                  | 295  |

## I. INTRODUCTORY.

ALL things must have a beginning, and our city of New York, now so rich and great, began in a very small way indeed. If we had been at the Battery on the eighteenth day of March, away back in 1524, we should probably have seen there a group of savages clad in skins, with bows in their hands, and a quiver full of arrows slung over their shoulders, intently watching a white speck that became larger every moment. Very soon it grew into a birdlike thing that swept on as gracefully as a swan. It was the first white man's sail the Indians had ever seen—that of the *Dolphin*, belonging to his Majesty Francis I., King of France, and sailed by a brave sailor and discoverer, Jean Verrazano of Florence.

The discovery of America by Columbus, thirty-two years before, had aroused the cupidity as well as the curiosity of the seafaring nations of Europe,—the English, Spanish, Dutch, French, and Portuguese,—and they were now sending out ships and sailors to discover, explore, and take possession of the new land. They thought, in their ignorance, that this land was a part of India, and that all the treasures of India were hidden in its savage and unknown interior.

Verrazano was one of these discoverers who had been

sent out by the King of France. If he followed the usual course of such adventurers on discovering a new country, he landed in state, with standard and cross, father confessor and men at arms, and planting the

Manhattan Island in the Sixteenth Century.

cross and the royal arms of France, he stood beside the cross with head bared, and repeated a formula by which he took possession of the entire country in the name of his royal master. He then sailed away, making no attempt to settle the new land. Nor was any ever made by Francis, who soon became engaged in war with the Emperor Charles V., King of Spain—a war which ended in the utter defeat of Francis at Pavia, and in his being carried a prisoner to Spain. Any title he might have had to our shores by virtue of his first discovery lapsed because of his failure to settle them.

Nearly a hundred years passed before another vessel

sailed into our bay—at least, so far as we have any record. But at last, on a mellow autumn day in September, 1609, a clumsy, odd-looking craft entered the Narrows and anchored in the mouth of the river. She had a stern much higher than her bows, a high, carved prow, and carried square sails on the two masts of a schooner; she flew a peculiar flag, new to the nations, of three horizontal stripes, orange, white, and blue—the Dutch flag. The name *Half Moon* was painted on her stern.

Before describing her mission it is necessary to say a word or two of the people who had sent her out. The Dutch were descended from those rude tribes, the Belgæ, Batavi, and Frisians, of whom Cæsar speaks. Later the conquering Franks and Saxons introduced a more refined and intellectual stock, which had grown to wealth and power under the successive rule of the wise Charlemagne, the lords and bishops of the feudal ages, and the strong kings of the house of Burgundy. Next these states came under the rule of Charles V., and of his son and successor, Philip II., the latter of whom governed them so harshly that seven provinces, a few years before our story opens, revolted and formed a republic.

Philip sought to subdue them, and a long and bitter war followed, which had been closed six months before the *Half Moon* sailed, by a truce of twelve years signed by both parties. You can read all about it in Mr. Motley's interesting work, "The Rise of the Dutch Republic."

The Dutch government was republican in form, but far more complex than is our own system. The genius of the country was almost wholly commercial, but it was a nation of great merchants, not shopkeepers; its trade extended over the known earth; it had on the seas at this time three thousand ships and one hundred thousand sailors, and enjoyed a trade of sixteen millions of pounds per annum—far more than England's, which was but six millions. Its East India Company, founded to secure the trade of India and the East, was the richest and greatest trading company then on the globe. It had a rival in the English East India Company, which had been chartered nine years before, and which, though not then so strong, was destined in a few years to supplant it. Both companies were very anxious to find a short passage to India. Such a passage was believed to extend around the northern shores of Europe and Asia. The Dutch company had fitted out the *Half Moon* to discover it, but had, strangely enough, given her in charge of an Englishman, a famous navigator of those times, named Henry Hudson.

Hudson, as you will find, was not here for settlement, but as a discoverer, an adventurer. He ascended the Hudson nearly to Albany, stopped to trade at various points with the Indians, returned, and sailed out of the Narrows again, leaving his own name to our noble river, the Hudson. Two years later, in 1611, the great Dutch navigator Adriaen Block sailed through Long Island Sound, discovering the shores of Connecticut and visiting Manhattan Island, which had been thus named from the tribe of Indians living on it. Block published a very graphic account of his voyage; but the haughty East India Company, having failed to find a passage to India through the new continent, took no further interest in it.

There were some shrewd merchants in Amsterdam, however, not shareholders in the East India Company, who saw what a rich trade in furs and other merchandise might be built up with the new country, and they formed a trading company, which was chartered by the States-General, the executive or working branch of the Dutch government. They built a fort and trading house on Manhattan Island, and another on an island in the Hudson near the present site of Albany.

Their charter was limited to three years, counting from January 1, 1615, and although they enjoyed a profitable trade, they made no permanent settlement. This charter is noteworthy from the fact that in it the country was first called New Netherlands.

But in Amsterdam a company was assuming form that was destined to effect both settlement and conquest. It was of slow growth, because many people objected to granting it a charter conferring such enormous powers as its promoters asked for; but at last, on June 3, 1621, the very year the truce with Spain ended, the States-General chartered it under the name of the West India Company.

Perhaps no body of merchants was ever invested with such enormous powers and privileges as this company possessed. It was a private company, and yet in many respects a sovereign state. It could contract alliances, declare war, make peace, administer justice, appoint or dismiss governors, judges, and servants, build forts, ships, cities—in fact, do anything necessary to promote trade and secure stability. To these powers was added a monopoly of the trade for the Atlantic coasts of Africa and America. Its leaders promised not only to carry on trade, but to attack Spain in her American colonies and to capture her ships on the high seas, and for this reason were given such extensive powers. It had a capital of twelve million florins (nearly five million dollars of our money), and its affairs were managed by five chambers, or boards, distributed among the different cities of Holland, the chamber of Amsterdam being the most important. The States-General further gave it a grant of the whole magnificent territory discovered by Hudson, on condition that it "should advance the peopling of it."

The company erected this grant into a province and committed its affairs to the chamber of Amsterdam, while the other chambers were to devote their attention to prosecuting the war against Spain; and very successful they were, too, capturing Bahia in 1624, the "great silver fleet," conveying treasure from the South American mines, in 1628, and the rich city of Pernambuco in 1630. All Netherlands rang with their exploits.

Meantime, reminded by jealous rivals, the Amsterdam chamber did not forget the savage island and the "fruitful and unsettled parts" in the West, that its charter obliged it to settle, but made an attempt at settlement by sending out thirty Walloons to New Netherlands, directing that eight should remain and found a trading post at Manhattan, while the remaining twenty-two should go up the Hudson to Fort Nassau, near Albany, and make a settlement there. This was in 1624, and these Walloons, residents of the frontier between France and Flanders, and distinguished for their valor and military spirit, were the first settlers of our great city. Next year, however, the company set about its task in earnest, advertising for "adventurers" to the New World, and offering free passage, employment, and other inducements, insomuch that, toward the close of the year, three large ships and a "yacht" sailed for Manhattan, carrying forty-five men, women, and children, with household goods, farming tools, and one hundred and three head of cattle. At the same time the company began framing a government for the new colony, and appointed a "director," or, as we should say, a governor, for it.

## II. THE DUTCH DYNASTY—PETER MINUIT.

THE director chosen was Peter Minuit of Wesel in Westphalia, an old servant of the East India Company. He had had experience in governing new countries, and this, with a kind, conciliating disposition and an inborn faculty for governing, made him one of the very best persons for the place that could have been chosen. He left Amsterdam in December, 1625, in a ship called the *Sea Mew* and bearing a large number of colonists. With great joy the busy settlers at Manhattan on May 4, 1626, beheld her furl sail and come to anchor off the Battery. A very different aspect the island presented to Minuit from that it now bears. Primeval forests hid the Jersey shore and the outline of Manhattan. A range of low, craggy hills covered with forests stretched through the center of the island from the Battery to Spuyten Duyvil. There were pretty grassy valleys between, and along the shores wide marshes stretched away to the north. At the present Canal Street

Marhattan

they extended quite across the island, so that at very high tides the waters of the East River flowed over into the Hudson. In sheltered valleys under the crags were the cornfields and bark wigwams of the Indians and the rude log cabins of the settlers. Cow paths crossed the marshes and wound in and out between the crags, often penetrating dense thickets of blackberry vines, creepers, grapevines, and bushes. Wolves, bears, and panthers lurked in these recesses. In their letters home the people often complained of the deer and wild turkeys that broke in and ate up their crops.

As his first step Minuit had been directed to purchase the island of its Indian owners. He therefore called a conference of the chiefs and head men, probably before he disembarked his company. You will find in Diedrich Knickerbocker's "History of New York" a very amusing account of the transaction; but Knickerbocker's sense of humor often played havoc with his historical accuracy. The scene as it actually occurred lacked no element of the strange and picturesque. On one side were the Hollanders, in long-skirted coats, some loose, some girt at the waist with a military sash, velvet breeches ending at the knee in black Holland stockings, and on their feet high military boots with wide-spreading tops. Their black hats of felt were low in the crown, with wide brims which were looped up, with rosettes or not at the fancy of the wearer. A short sword was suspended in a sash drawn over the right shoulder and passing under the left arm, but otherwise the Hollanders were without weapons. Opposed to these stern, warlike men were the unkempt, long-haired savages, clad in deerskins or waist belts of woven grass. Between the two stood a great sea chest with the lid open, revealing therein ribbons, beads, buttons, gayly embroidered coats, and similar articles, which were taken out one by one and shown the delighted savages, who were only too glad to give their island in

Purchase of Manhattan Island.

exchange for the glittering baubles. We can hardly believe that the ground on which our opulent city now stands was first bought for goods worth twenty-four dollars of our money.

In the midst of savage and fief Minuit now set up his orderly government. It was unique in many respects, quite different from that of the New England colonies on the east, who lived under charters granted by the King of England and had their own legislature, which, being composed of men elected by themselves, acted as a check on the royal governor. The director, himself the servant of the company, enjoyed absolute power, except that he could not inflict the death penalty. The people had also the right of appeal to the home chamber, and from its decision to the States-General. An advisory council of five of the wisest men of the colony was also to be appointed by the governor, to whose advice he was to give due weight. There were but two other officers of the colony, the secretary of the council and the schout fiscal, the latter as great a figure in the early history of Manhattan as the director himself; for he was State's attorney, sheriff, constable, and tax collector, and beadle and tithingman on Sundays. He began the Lord's day by preceding the members of the council to church, and during divine service patrolled the streets to see that no tapster profaned the

New Amsterdam.

day by selling schnapps, and no negro slave or Indian by gaming.

The people in general were mere fiefs, or servants, of the company. They could not own land; they could not trade with the Indians or among themselves; they could make nothing, not even what they wore or consumed, these privileges being reserved for the company. After some thirty small cabins had been built along the East River, Minuit and his engineer, Kryn Fredericke, built a fort on a slight elevation near where Broadway now enters the Battery, and called it Fort Amsterdam. Then the busy delvers opened quarries in the neighboring crags, and built of the "Manhattan stone" found there a warehouse for the company's stores and other property. They do not seem to have had the tools for building a windmill after the fashion of their fathers, and so built a horse mill for grinding grain. For a church they fitted up the loft of the horse mill. Minister they had none, but the company had sent over two zeikentroosters, or "consolers of the sick" (what we would call lay readers), who read to them from the Bible on Sundays. But in two years a regularly ordained minister, the Rev. Jonas Michaelis, arrived, and the little colony was complete. It had taken eighteen years to found the settlement.

Minuit next turned his attention to trading with the Indians, and sent a little fleet, composed of a sloop, the ship's jolly-boat, and canoes, up the Hudson into every bay and creek where an Indian lodge could be seen, exchanging axes, knives, beads, and gay fabrics for furs and wampum, and inviting the savages to come down to the fort and trade with their white brothers. Many came, and soon tall, gaunt savages in skins or blankets, laden with bales of fur, venison, turkeys, wild fowl, and other game, became familiar objects in the streets of New Amsterdam; for so Minuit had named his infant settlement. Very soon about the company's warehouse there was a great bustle of trade indeed, earnest of the forthcoming greatness of the port.

When the good ship *Arms of Amsterdam* sailed for home, September 23, 1626, she bore "7,246 beaver skins, 178½ otter skins, 675 otter skins, 48 minck skins, 36 wild-cat skins, 33 minck skins, 34 rat skins, and great store of oak and hickory timber," the whole valued at forty-five thousand guilders, or some nineteen thousand dollars. She also took specimens of the "summer grain" the colonists had just harvested, viz., rye, oats, barley, wheat, beans, flax, buckwheat, and canary seed. She carried, too, news of the birth of Sarah Rapalje, the "first-born Christian daughter" in New Netherlands, born June 9, 1625.

Minuit knew that the English had settled on Massachusetts Bay, and he soon sent letters to Governor Bradford at Plymouth, proposing trade. The governor replied very courteously, saying that at present they had need of nothing, but that in the future they might, "if the rates were reasonable." At the same time he gently intimated that the Dutch were on English soil unlawfully; for England claimed the whole country between New England and Virginia west to the Pacific by virtue of the earlier discoveries of her sea captains, Cabot, John Smith, and others. On a receipt of this

Minuit sent his beloved secretary, Isaac de Rasières, in the bark *Nassau*, with many presents, who came to Plymouth, was well received by Governor Bradford, and spent many days in the village, being treated "with courtesy and rare good will" by the Pilgrims, and laying the foundation for a flourishing trade between the two colonies.

New Amsterdam prospered, however, without English trade. Six bouweries, or farms, were opened by the company in the open meadows along the East River, and stocked with sheep, cattle, hogs, and goats, while additional colonists were constantly arriving from the fatherland. In 1628 there were two hundred and seventy inhabitants. By 1629 the exports had risen to one hundred and thirty thousand guilders, and the imports to one hundred and thirteen thousand (about $45,200). But neither this progress nor the promise of future revenues satisfied the directors at home, and after some thought they hit upon a plan which promised larger and quicker returns. Among their stockholders were many wealthy merchants who, they thought, would prize a title and an estate. To each of them the directors said in effect: "If you will at your own expense establish a colony in our territory of New Netherlands we will grant you these privileges: a title, that of patroon, or feudal chief; an estate, stretching for sixteen miles along one bank of the river, or for eight along both banks, and extending inland as far as you can explore; exempt you and your people from taxation for ten years; grant you free trade, except in furs, which we reserve for ourselves, and full property rights; protect you from enemies, and supply you with servants. You shall forever possess and enjoy these lands, with the fruits, rights, minerals, rivers, and fountains, the fishing and fowling and grinding, the supreme authority and jurisdiction; and if you found cities, you shall have authority to establish for them officers and magistrates. In return you must agree to satisfy the Indians for the land taken; to plant a colony of at least fifty souls above fifteen years of age within four years; to provide a minister and schoolmaster for the colony as soon as possible, and until that is done a comforter of the sick. You may take up the lands anywhere except on Manhattan Island, which we reserve for ourselves."

Several directors and others accepted these terms, and thus came into being those great feudal manors and patroonships along the Hudson, which after the Revolution caused much trouble and discord, because in conflict with the spirit of the age. At the time they were given, however, they wrought both good and evil: good because they provided schools and churches, settled men in strong, well-ordered villages, and satisfied the Indian for his lands; bad in that they introduced human slavery, monopoly of land, and aristocratic privilege.

The first great patroonship created by this act was that of Rensselaerwyck, founded in 1630 by Kiliaen Van Rensselaer, a pearl merchant of Amsterdam and a director. By successive purchases of the Indians he became master of a territory twenty-four miles long by forty-eight wide, of an estimated area of seven hundred thousand acres. Later it made two counties, Albany and Rensselaer, and part of another, Columbia. Michael de

Pauw, another director, finding the best lands on the Hudson taken, purchased in June, 1630, the territory called Hoboken-Hacking, across the Hudson from New Amsterdam, and the next month Staten Island and the country south of his first purchase, now known as Jersey City. But these purchases, which included the more desirable of the company's lands, aroused the jealousy of the other directors who had secured none, and to appease them four others were admitted to a share in Rensselaerwyck. Settlers, horses, and cattle were soon sent to the latter, and in a few years it was a flourishing village. Pauw founded on his grant a village which he called the " Commune," and which no doubt gave its name to the later Communipaw.

But the company very soon found that the patroons were more intent on trading with the Indians than on clearing and cultivating their lands, and especially that they were buying and selling furs, which trade had been reserved as the exclusive right of the company, and a bitter quarrel arose over the matter which greatly hindered the growth of the colony. So violent did it become that it was carried to their High Mightinesses the States-General, who passed laws restricting the privileges of the patroons. Minuit had ratified the patroons' grants, and, it was charged, had in other ways favored them at the expense of the company, and this, with some minor charges of extravagance, led to his recall. He sailed for Holland in the ship *Eendracht*, in the spring of 1632. He had governed the infant settlement for six years, in general, it must be admitted, with wisdom, sagacity, and prudence.

## III. WOUTER VAN TWILLER.

AND now the directors sat in their great oak-paneled chamber in Amsterdam to choose a new governor. After much debate they fixed on Wouter Van Twiller as the man. You may have read in Diedrich Knickerbocker's "History of New York" that author's famous description of him. "He was exactly five feet six inches in height and six feet five inches in circumference. His head was a perfect sphere, and of such stupendous dimensions that Dame Nature, with all her sex's ingenuity, would have been puzzled to construct a neck capable of supporting it; wherefore she wisely declined the attempt, and settled it firmly on the top of his backbone just between the shoulders. His body was oblong and particularly capacious at bottom. His legs were short, but sturdy in proportion to the weight they had to sustain; so that, when erect, he had not a little the appearance of a beer barrel on skids."

But, burlesque aside, Van Twiller was a grotesque figure, a mountain of flesh, slow and narrow of mind, with a petty spirit, and a burgomaster's fondness for good dinners and sound wine. He owed his selection to the powerful patroon Kiliaen Van Rensselaer, whose niece he had married, and who desired for govenor a person attached to his interests.

Van Twiller arrived early in April, 1633. As the ship's boat bore him and his retinue ashore, he saw, collected on the rude wharf, between two and three hundred men and women with stolid Dutch faces, the former clad in baggy, homespun breeches and loose blouses well worn and toil-stained, the latter in kerchiefs and short gowns; behind them a group of Indians looking curiously on; and beyond these crags and the somber forest, with here and there a clearing or cornfield.

The director's party took up its quarters in the fort, in the houses vacated by Minuit. One day soon after his arrival, as he sat with one of the newly arrived patroons, De Vries, on the fort parapet, smoking and chatting, he saw a vessel pass the Narrows and come up the bay with all sail set, round to, and anchor under the guns of the fort. Her straight lines and clean, shipshape appearance would have proclaimed her nationality even if the red cross of England had not flown at her peak. Quickly she dispatched a boat ashore in charge of an officer in resplendent scarlet uniform.

"What ship is that?" growled the director, as the boat grounded.

"The *William* of London, and last from Boston," replied the officer, doffing his hat and making a profound bow.

"Who commands?" continued the director.

"Jacob Eelkens," was the reply.

"I know the varlet," said De Vries, aside, "he was post trader at Fort Orange for the first company, and was discharged for petty thieving. Have a care, your Excellency."

"What doeth he here?" continued the director.

"Prithee, he would trade with the savage," replied the envoy.

Van Twiller frowned. Here was the old vexed question of English rights again; like Banquo's ghost, it would not down.

"He hath sent me to present his compliments," continued the officer, "and to invite your Excellency and the honorable councilors to dine with him to-morrow. He bade me say there shall be no lack of good wine and ale."

"Do not go," said De Vries; but Van Twiller had a weakness for the pleasures of the table, and accepted. Accordingly, next day two boats conveyed him, his councilors, and De Vries to the *William*, where they were received with due state and ceremony. At the dinner which followed, we have it on the authority of De Vries, the songs and mad capers of Van Twiller in his cups did grievously discredit the Dutch government and caused the English to laugh at his authority.

After lying five days before the fort Eelkens coolly announced that he should proceed to Fort Orange and trade with his old friends the Mohawks there. The conduct of Van Twiller on receiving this startling news shows the character of the man. He invited the whole crew of the *William* into the fort, and to overawe them ran up the tricolored flag, and fired a salute in honor of the Prince of Orange. But Eelkens, so far from being frightened, laughed and sent his gunner on board the *William*, with orders to fire a whole broadside in honor of King Charles; then, while the guns were still thundering, he hurried aboard with his crew, weighed anchor, and sailed up the river, his men twirling their thumbs at the Dutch, who stood petrified with astonishment, making no attempt to hinder them. Van Twiller was the first to recover his wits. He called for a barrel of wine, broached it, and invited the entire populace—which had come running to the spot on the sound of the guns—to join him in drinking it; then, made valiant by the wine, he swung his hat and shouted: "All ye who love the Prince of Orange and me, emulate me in this, and aid me in repelling the violence of that Englishman."

As soon as possible three armed vessels were made ready, and, with one hundred and four men at arms on board, the director stood up the river in pursuit. In the meantime Eelkens had arrived at a point about a mile below Fort Orange (Albany), where he raised a marquee, landed his cargo, and began a profitable trade with the Mohawks, who were delighted to meet again their old friend and ally. News of his invasion was quickly carried to Houten, the Dutch official in charge of Fort Orange, and he hastened down in his shallop, "wreathed in green boughs, with a trumpeter making stirring music," and set up a rival booth beside the interloper's, and did what he could to disparage his wares and hinder his trade. But Eelkens had new and superior goods, purchased with full knowledge of what the Indians required, and was fast disposing of his cargo when, fourteen days after his arrival, the Dutch fleet, which we left at New Amsterdam, hove in sight.

As soon as its commander could secure the aid of the soldiers in Fort Orange he sailed down to the English marquee, and commanded Eelkens to take his goods and begone forthwith. But the trader not responding so quickly as he wished, he ordered his men to beat and disperse the Indians who were trading with him; then, unheeding Eelkens's protests that he was on English soil and had a right to trade there, they pulled his tent about his ears, and hurried his goods on board the *William*, "sounding in their boat meantime a trumpet in disgrace of the English." Then they escorted the *William* to the mouth of the river, or, to use Eelkens's words: "The Dutch came along with us in their shallop, and they sticked green bowes all about her, and drank strong waters, and sounded their trumpet in a triumphing manner over us." Thus a second time the English were defeated in asserting their claim to the Hudson; but in the end they triumphed, as we shall see.

Van Twiller soon had a deeper quarrel on his hands, this time with the English of Plymouth and Massachusetts Bay. Both nations laid claim to the Connecticut River and its rich valley lands, the Dutch by virtue of Block's discovery, the English by grant of their king. To strengthen their claim, the Dutch, in 1632, had purchased of the Indians the lands near the mouth of the river, and Van Twiller now sent his commissary, Jacob Van Curler, to buy a large tract on the upper river, on the site of the present city of Hartford, and further built there a trading post armed with two cannon, calling it the House of Good Hope. The English met this by establishing settlements on the Connecticut, whereupon Van Twiller sent an armed force of seventy men to clear the river; but they returned without striking a blow, finding the English " very warlike, and the woods full of painted savages." This ended the doughty governor's campaigns against the English on the Connecticut, though both he and his successors continued to assert their claim to the " Great River."

In conducting the internal affairs of his little kingdom Van Twiller was more fortunate. He had some trouble with the powerful patroons, but no serious difficulty; he placated the Indians; he erected many public buildings and works, and he saw new farms and villages springing up about him. The patroon Pietersen de Vries purchased Staten Island and founded a colony there. The Walloon settlement, the first on the present site of Brooklyn, grew apace. Van Twiller completed Fort Amsterdam, and built a substantial dwelling of brick within it for himself, a parsonage and stables also for the Domine Bogardus, a country house for himself on his plantation, a brewery and boathouse, several mills, and dwellings for the smith, cooper, corporal, and other officers, all at the expense of the company. But when his bills were presented the directors objected, and partly on this account, partly because of charges made by De Vries and others that he was diverting the moneys of the company to his own use, the directors removed him, and appointed in his place Wilhelm Kieft, who took the oath of office at Amsterdam, September 2, 1637.

## IV. WILHELM KIEFT.

AS soon as news of this reached New Amsterdam the people there began to talk about Kieft. They said he had become bankrupt as a merchant in Holland, and had been condemned to have his portrait fixed to the gallows, and when later he had been minister to Turkey he had kept the funds sent him to ransom Christian captives from the Turk, and left them to languish in captivity. They whispered such things as the new governor and his party stepped from the bark *Blessing*, on the 28th of March, 1638. The bystanders saw a little man with sharp, pinched features, a cold gray eye, a furtive, suspicious look and autocratic air; a man of good natural abilities, but undisciplined, of peppery temper, selfish, conceited, and tyrannical; the very man to embroil himself with his subjects, and his subjects with their neighbors. This he proceeded to do with great facility. He made oppressive and vexatious sumptuary laws,—that is, laws directing what the people should eat and what they should drink, and when they should sleep,—and as he enforced them with great rigor the whole colony was soon up in arms against him. Not liking the check imposed on him by the council, he dissolved it by a trick. The directors had given him the power of fixing the number of men in this council, and he now limited it to one, and then ordained that his council should have but one vote in the government, while he had two. This practically made him dictator, for the right of appeal to Amsterdam was very little used because of the distance, delay, and expense. Next he embroiled himself and the colony with the Indians by making a law that they should pay tribute, and when they refused tried to compel them by force. The result was what a wiser man would have foreseen. The people openly violated the oppressive laws, and very soon Kieft had an Indian war on his hands, a state of affairs which the former governors had sought above all things to avoid.

One day in 1640 word came that some swine running at large in the forests of Staten Island were missing, and the director, without inquiry, charged that the Raritan Indians had stolen them, and sent out a company of troops with orders to kill, burn, and destroy. Glad of the opportunity, the soldiers hurried into the Raritan country, burned their villages and cornfields, and only refrained from killing the Indians because they could not find them. In revenge the Raritans descended on the bouwery of the innocent, humane De Vries on Staten Island, killed four of his planters, and burned his house and tobacco barn. At this, frenzied with rage, Kieft offered his allies, the River Indians, ten fathoms of wampum for every head of a Raritan, and twenty fathoms each for the heads of the murderers of the planters. This set hundreds of human hounds on the trail, and in a few days Pacham, chief of the Tankitikes, who lived about Sing Sing, came in with the head of the chief who had slain De Vries's men dangling at the end of a stick. At the same time the Raritans came in and begged for mercy. A few weeks after it was learned that the swine had been taken by a party of the company's servants on their way to Virginia.

On another morning, Claes Smit, the village wheelwright, who lived alone in a little house in the suburbs, was found murdered in his bed, and it was discovered that he had been killed by a Weckquaesgeck Indian whose uncle had been slain by negro slaves of the company twenty years before, and who had waited thus long for an opportunity to make the blood atonement which Indian custom laid on the next of kin in such cases. Kieft promptly demanded the murderer from the Weckquaesgeck chief, but the latter refused. He was sorry, he said, that twenty Christians had not been killed. The blood of his relative cried from the ground for vengeance, and was not yet appeased.

Kieft would have marched an army against the tribe at once, but was deterred by the protests and threats of De Vries and other leaders, who reminded him that they were two hundred and fifty men at arms against ten thousand savages, and asked him if he wished to provoke a general Indian war.

Alarmed at the turn affairs had taken, the director now called a meeting of the patroons and head men, and asked their advice. The latter, quick to take advantage of the occasion, chose a council of twelve wise men to advise the director in this and other emergencies, much to the latter's disgust. In the present case they advised against declaring war at once, for three reasons: their cattle were still in the woods, their crops unharvested, and their people scattered about on the farms; in the winter, they said, these conditions would not exist. Kieft therefore staid the uplifted battle-ax, though sorely against his will.

In January the twelve gave their consent, and at the same time called his attention to certain evils and abuses in his government which they hoped would be remedied; they also asked for certain concessions to popular rights, a council being one of them. Kieft received them kindly and promised fairly, but a day or two after issued a proclamation dissolving the council, which he said had been called to consult on the Indian crisis, which now being done, he thanked them for their trouble, and would make use of their advice "with God's help and fitting time." The paper concluded by sternly forbidding further meetings, which "tended to the great injury both of the country and of our authority."

Being now again supreme ruler, the director ordered Hendrik Van Dyck, his ensign, to march with eighty soldiers against the Weckquaesgecks and harry them with fire and sword. The valiant ensign and his party set out with stout hearts, but became entangled in the vast forests, and returned without having seen a Weckquaesgeck. The campaign served its purpose, however, for the savages, hearing of the danger they had barely escaped, came in and sued for mercy.

Kieft now became even more reckless and arbitrary in his government, disdaining all counsel, insomuch that in 1643 the infant settlement was confronted with a general

Indian war. The River Indians, the Connecticut and Long Island tribes, formed an alliance to destroy the Dutch, fifteen hundred savages against two hundred and fifty white men. Soon the outlying farms and villages were attacked and burned, and such of the inhabitants as were not killed sent flying to the fort for safety. In this crisis Kieft acted like one bereft of reason; he sent his soldiers up the Hudson and into Connecticut and Long Island with orders to slaughter the Indians, men, women, and children, wherever they could be found, to burn their villages and destroy their cornfields. Murders most inhuman were committed under his orders, and all the murders were avenged either then, or later by the allied tribes.

Meantime petition after petition had been sent to the home company detailing Kieft's crimes and unjust acts,

Stadt Huys.

and praying for his recall; but so powerful was the influence of the great patroon Van Rensselaer with the directors that for a long time no notice of them was taken. At length, in the spring of 1645, the colonists threatened to leave in a body unless he was recalled, and this, together with the influence of the wise and humane patroon De Vries, who had returned to Holland in disgust, led the chamber to remove Kieft and appoint Petrus Stuyvesant in his place. Over against the evil that Kieft wrought may be set much good that he did; for he certainly did much to make Manhattan more beautiful and habitable. He repaired the fort, erected public buildings, set out orchards and gardens and encouraged others to do so, straightened the streets and made laws for keeping them cleaner. One of his buildings was the great stone tavern which later became the Stadt Huys, or City Hall, and he began and nearly finished, within the fort, the large stone church which was for many years the city's only house of worship.

## V. PETRUS STUYVESANT.

IT was over two years before a new governor came, so that long before his arrival his personal history, character, and appearance had been described and canvassed. He was a native of Friesland, it was said, son of a clergyman there. Bred to the profession of arms, he had early entered the service of the West India Company, and won renown in those brilliant battles, sieges, naval combats, and predatory descents on the Spanish-American coasts, which gained glory for the company and abundantly filled its coffers. Later, as governor of Curaçao, he undertook to conquer the island of Saint Martin, but having lost a leg in the action, he returned to Holland for surgical advice; and the directors, being then in search of a governor for their mismanaged colony, fixed upon this victorious commander and martinet.

The people of Manhattan were not very well pleased with his appointment; they feared he would be as tyrannical as Kieft, and regarded his selection as proof that the company meant to continue its despotic form of government. However, anything was to be preferred to their present condition, and they waited hopefully for the coming of their new master. He arrived on the 11th of May, 1647, with a fleet of four large ships and a noble company : his beautiful and accomplished wife, his widowed sister, Mrs. Bayard, and her three boys, a vice director, a council which had been appointed by the chamber in Amsterdam as a check on the director, men at arms, and colonists. The fleet had been on the way since Christmas, having made a detour to the West Ind es on some affair of Stuyvesant's.

As the director came to land, the fort thundered a salute, the people waved hats and handkerchiefs, and Kieft, advancing, read an address of welcome, to which the new ruler responded.

Neither his words nor his manner pleased the people; the latter, they said, seemed too much like that of a prince addressing conquered subjects. In his speech he said to them : " I shall be in my government as a father over his children, for the advantage of the privileged West India Company, the burghers, and the country."

Stuyvesant assumed the reins of government on the 27th of May, and his words and manner on that occasion were still less to their liking. " He kept the people standing more than an hour with their heads uncovered, while he wore his chapeau as though he were the Czar of Muscovy," said an eyewitness. At the same time he announced his council, which had been appointed in Holland, as we have seen. The former secretary and schout fiscal were retained; two new offices had been created, a master of equipage and an English secretary and interpreter. He further told them that the company had established a court of justice, of which Van Dinclage was to be judge, but from whose decisions an appeal might be taken to himself.

Stuyvesant ruled with a high hand. Almost his first official act showed the people that they could expect little more liberty under him than under Kieft. There was living in New Amsterdam at this time a very respectable gentleman named Cornelis Melyn, who had been president of that council which had been appointed by the patroons and chief men under Kieft. He had lost heavily in the Indian war at that time, and now, with Joachim Pietersen Kuyter, also a member of the same council, petitioned that the causes of that war might be inquired into, and that the testimony of citizens might be taken under oath.

Stuyvesant believed that the government should be upheld, right or wrong; he appointed the commission as desired, but himself went before it and said that in his opinion "the two malignant fellows were disturbers of the peace, and that it was treason to complain of one's magistrates, whether there was cause or not," whereupon the commission refused the petition. At this, Kieft, seeing that the director was on his side, had the two burghers arrested on a charge of "rebellion and sedition." Justice was pretty swift in those days, so the two unfortunates were quickly haled before the newly created court, where Stuyvesant sat with Judge Van Dinclage to try them. There were then no lawyers in New Netherlands, and the prisoners pleaded their own case, and did it ably too. They proved the truth of their charges against Kieft, and that in making them they were not moved by vindictive motives. Yet in spite of this, and against law and evidence, the judges declared them guilty. Melyn declared that he would appeal to the States-General. This threw Stuyvesant into a violent rage. He stamped about on his wooden leg, with "the foam on his beard," and said to Melyn: "Were I persuaded that you would bring this matter before their High Mightinesses, I would have you hanged on the highest tree in New Netherlands." Next he pronounced sentence: for Melyn seven years' banishment and a fine of three hundred guilders, and for Kuyter banishment for three years and a fine of one hundred and fifty guilders.

A few days after the trial the banished men were put aboard the ship *Princess*, bound for Holland. With them sailed over one hundred souls. Kieft was among them, and Domine Bogardus, with many who were dissatisfied with the government as administered by the new director. But the *Princess* was wrecked in a great storm on the wild Welsh coast. Kieft and Domine Bogardus went down in the swirling waters. Only Melyn, Kuyter, and some eighteen others escaped.

When Melyn and Kuyter, after long delay, brought their case before the States-General, Stuyvesant's judgment was revoked, and Melyn and Kuyter were sent back with a summons to him from the Prince of Orange and the States-General ordering him to appear and answer before them, either in person or by his attorney; but the matter seems to have been compounded, as we hear no more of it.

The great event of Stuyvesant's reign, save perhaps the last, was the granting of the charter which made New Amsterdam a city, and which was given in 1652, in answer to repeated complaints and petitions of the citizens. It was on the plan of the ancient charter of old Amsterdam, which provided for the election by the people of a schout, four burgomasters, nine schepens, and an advisory council of thirty-six men. The first fourteen constituted a body similar to the English mayor and common council, and made and executed the laws by which the city was governed. They were also a court for the trial of civil and criminal cases. In this charter of New Amsterdam, however, the company limited the number of burgomasters to two and of schepens to five, but declared expressly that they should be elected by the people.

Stuyvesant, however, largely nullified the charter by appointing the city fathers instead of allowing the people to elect them, and after he had appointed them told them plainly that he should preside at their meetings whenever he deemed it necessary, and advise them in matters of importance. And so with an autocratic, self-willed military commander as governor, the people found the piece of parchment of little avail. They had the shadow of self-government, however, if not the substance.

The old stone tavern built by Kieft was cleaned, remodeled, and set apart as a stadt huys, or city hall, and there the burgomasters and schepens held their sessions.

Stuyvesant proclaimed the city on the 2d of February, 1653. It then comprised some fifteen hundred inhabitants and about three hundred houses, mostly of wood, with a few of stone. It had no trade of its own, and there was scarcely cleared land enough about it to supply it with vegetables. Is it not wonderful that in two centuries and a half this village has grown to be the metropolis of the western continent and the second

City of New Amsterdam. 1653.

largest city in the world? In 1654 Stuyvesant presented the city with its long-delayed seal, the occasion being a banquet held in the council chamber by the burgomasters and schepens on the eve of his departure for a visit of ceremony to the West Indies. The guests all crowded round to view it. It bore the arms of old Amsterdam, three crosses saltire, with a beaver for a crest, and above, on the mantle, the initial letters C. W. I. C., meaning the " Chartered West India Company." Within a wreath of laurel was the legend, *Sigillum Amstelodamensis in Novo Belgio* (" Seal of Amsterdam in New Belgium ").

Stuyvesant returned in July, and shortly after,

under orders from Holland, embarked with an army of seven hundred men to drive off certain Swedes who, in Minuit's time, had settled on the banks of the South River, on lands claimed by the Dutch. A few days after the fleet sailed, the ex-sheriff, Van Dyck, discovered an Indian woman stealing peaches in his orchard, and shot her dead on the spot. Her people at once sent swift runners to all the river tribes, to the Connecticut and Long Island Indians, praying for vengeance, and apprising them that the director and all the able-bodied men of the city were absent.

The savages at once sprang to arms, and just before daybreak on September 15, 1655, appeared before the city in sixty-four canoes bearing nineteen hundred warriors. They quickly spread through the town, and broke into a few houses on pretense of looking for hostile Indians, but really to see if the murderer Van Dyck was in the city. The burgomasters and schepens, aroused, went among them, gathered the chiefs into the fort, and with soothing and persuasive words induced them to draw their men out of the city. They retired to Nutten (now Governors) Island, but quickly returned, hurried to the house of Van Dyck, and killed him. The schepen, Van der Grist, who lived next door, hastened to the sheriff's aid, and was stricken down with an ax. By this time the alarm had been given; the burgher guard sprang to arms, and drove the Indians off, killing several.

Stung to fury by this loss, the savages hurried to Hoboken and Pavonia, across the Hudson, killed every person they could find, and ravaged the plantations, then hastened to the unfortunate settlements of De Vries on Staten Island, where the same scenes were enacted—a heavy price to pay for one man's rash and cruel act.

Stuyvesant had just received the submission of the Swedes when a courier brought the news of this Indian foray, whereupon he returned at once, but acted with much more wisdom than Kieft had shown on a similar occasion. He called the chiefs together, and by kind words and presents allayed their just resentment and restored confidence.

The later years of Stuyvesant's term were marked by religious persecution, before unknown in New Netherlands. "Allow all the free exercise of their religion in their own houses," had been the command of the company; but the director would recognize only the Dutch Reformed Church. He persecuted both the Lutherans of Holland and the Quakers and Baptists of New England. These and other cruelties so incensed the people that Stuyvesant had scarcely a friend in his government outside of his official family.

He was very soon to feel the effect of this hostility. England, as we have remarked, had never yielded her claim to the territory covered by New Netherlands. By the year 1664 she believed the time had come for gathering it to herself.

All through the reign of Stuyvesant events had been leading up to this end. Charles I. of England had been deposed and beheaded. Cromwell had had his day as Protector, and after his death the monarchy had been restored in the person of Charles II., who was now king.

He was a weak man, and the management of foreign affairs had fallen largely into the hands of his abler brother James, the Duke of York, and of the strong, statesmanlike men whom the king had selected as his ministers. From the moment that Charles felt secure on his throne, aggressions against this little strip of Dutch territory began. In 1664, ignoring some former grants, Charles gave to his brother James the entire territory claimed by the Dutch; and at once that energetic nobleman set about getting possession of the grant, a work in which he had the active aid and encouragement of King Charles's ministers.

That the seizure might cause a war with Holland did not trouble him in the least; he disliked the Dutch for various reasons; besides, a war would focus national attention upon himself, and already he had his eye on the throne of England. Four men-of-war, the *Guinea* of thirty-six guns, the *Elias* of thirty, the *Martin* of sixteen, and the *William-and-Nicholas* of ten, were borrowed from the government, and, manned with four hundred and fifty men at arms, were placed under command of Colonel Richard Nicolls, a veteran officer and a courteous, humane gentleman.

This fleet left Portsmouth, England, about the middle of May, 1664, having on board a form of government and laws for the territory when it should be taken. So sure were they of capturing it that Nicolls bore orders to the governors of the New England colonies directing them to aid in the movement. The fleet reached Boston late in July, and its commander asked for the aid of Massachusetts and Connecticut in carrying out his design. Massachusetts had little love for King Charles, and responded somewhat tardily, but Connecticut, which had had a great deal of trouble with the Dutch on her western border, gladly aided the enterprise.

Stuyvesant was away on a visit to Fort Orange when news that the English were about to attack his capital reached him, and he at once hurried back. Twenty-four hours after reaching home, as he paced restlessly the parapet of the fort, he saw far down in the lower bay the dim outlines of a man-of-war from whose peak floated the red cross flag of Saint George; it was the *Guinea*, leading the fleet to the attack. Never before had a commander been caught so unprepared: there were no provisions for a siege; of the thirteen hundred pounds of powder in the fort six hundred were useless; of the garrison of one hundred and fifty regular soldiers and two hundred and fifty militia the director was not sure of the loyalty of one.

Stuyvesant fumed and stamped about on his wooden leg. He swore that he would hold the town against all odds, and he began active though tardy preparations for defense. He mustered his four hundred men, and ordered every third man among the citizens to repair to the defenses with spade, shovel, or wheelbarrow.

But the latter murmured at this. Was the director crazy, they asked, that he thought of defense? Suppose he held the fort, did he not know that the frigates could pass up the river and rake the town on either side?

Many refused to go. Perhaps a third of the population were English-speaking people, in sympathy with Nicolls, and these now went about the city spreading disaffection and working on the fears of the people. Nevertheless, Stuyvesant continued his preparations: he placed a guard at the city gates; he ordered the brewers to cease making grain into malt, and set his slaves to thrashing grain at his farm and conveying it to the fort.

Meantime the fleet anchored in the bay and sent a summons to the director to surrender. Stuyvesant called a council of the burgomasters and schepens, who advised delay and the sending of commissioners to argue the matter with the invaders. This was done. But Nicolls told them plainly that he was not come to argue, but to execute. The council then asked three days to consider, which was at once given, as it gave the humane commander the opportunity he desired. He took advantage of the delay to move his vessels abreast of Governors Island, where he disembarked five companies of soldiers and sent them to effect a junction with a party of horse and foot from Connecticut and Long Island, after which the allied force encamped on the Brooklyn shore by the present terminus of Fulton Ferry. Nicolls was very desirous of taking the place without bloodshed, as his object was to placate the Dutch and make them contented and orderly subjects of the King of England. He now issued a proclamation offering to all who would submit life, liberty, property, and the fullest enjoyment of every right whether of person or estate. This paper he distributed throughout the city by means of his agents, and awaited the result. The people read it or heard of it, and urged the director to submit; but he refused, and hurried on his preparations for defense.

The original demand had been made on Saturday, August 30. The three days' grace would expire on Wednesday morning, September 3. On Tuesday morning a rowboat was seen approaching from the fleet. It contained six dignified gentlemen of commanding presence, conspicuous among them the noble figure of Governor Winthrop of Connecticut, whom Stuyvesant had several times met at banquet board and council table—an embassy bent on effecting a bloodless surrender. They were met at the wharf with due courtesy, a salute being fired in their honor, and conducted to the Stadt Huys, where Stuyvesant and his council were waiting to receive them. Winthrop broached their mission, and with his well-known eloquence urged the director to give over a hopeless struggle and spare useless shedding of blood by yielding the city to the English.

But the lion-hearted director swore he would never submit. Winthrop then delivered a letter from Colonel Nicolls, which was read to the council, in which he promised that the Dutch should have full liberty equally with the king's subjects to settle in New Netherlands and to trade with their own country or return thither.

A great crowd of citizens had gathered outside to hear the result, and the burgomasters now asked that the letter might be read to them; but Stuyvesant, who feared its effect, refused. A war of words ensued, and in the midst of it the choleric director seized the letter and tore it to pieces. At this Cornelis Steenwyck, a member of the council, roundly denounced him, and with his fellow-officials quitted the place. On gaining the street they told the people what had taken place, and the latter presently deputed three prominent men among them to call upon the director and demand the letter. In reply the latter showed them the fragments, but on the delegates still demanding the letter, he went out to the people and tried to reason with them; but his voice was drowned in angry shouts for the letter.

"That," said Stuyvesant, "was addressed to the officers of government, and does not concern you." But the people were not to be placated, and amid bitter curses and threats Stuyvesant withdrew to the fort, while Nicholas Bayard, the politic courtier, pieced the torn fragments of the letter together, and from it made a copy which he read to the people, who were little appeased by it, and still clamored for submission. Meantime Stuyvesant, in the fort, was writing another letter to Nicolls, in which he gave an exhaustive account of the Dutch discovery and settlement of New Netherlands, and forcibly stated their claims to it. He sealed it and sent it by four of his most trusted friends.

"Nay," said Nicolls, when the envoys reached his ship, "I stand on no question of right; if my terms are not accepted I must carry out my orders and attack."

The delegates still wished to argue, but Nicolls cut them short. "On Thursday I shall speak with you at the Manhattans," he said significantly.

"Thou wilt be welcome if thou comest as a friend," replied the envoys.

"I will come with my ships and my soldiers, and he

will be a bold messenger who will dare to come on board and solicit terms," said Nicolls.

"What then is to be done?" they asked.

"Hoist the white flag over the fort, and I may take it into consideration," was the reply. He promised that he would not fire upon the city without warning, but refused their request not to move his troops nearer the city. "To-day I shall arrive at the ferry," he added; "to-morrow we can agree with one another."

That same day he landed three companies of regulars at Gravesend, and marched overland at their head to the Fulton Ferry, where he formed a junction with the troops already there. While this was being done two of the frigates sailed up past the fort with ports open and guns shotted, ready to pour in a broadside if its guns should open. Stuyvesant stood on the parapet as they passed, and would have ordered his gunners to fire, no doubt, for he was not lacking in courage, had not Domine Megapolensis at the critical moment laid his hand upon his shoulder. "It is madness," said he. "What can our twenty guns do against the sixty-two pointed toward us from yonder frigates? Will you be the first to shed blood?"

Once they were past, however, the director's resolution returned, and taking one hundred soldiers, he hurried up into the city to resist any attempt of the English to land. But as he came into the town he was met by a petition signed by ninety-three prominent citizens, including the magistrates and clergy, begging him to accept the generous terms of the English and save the city from burning, and the people from the sword.

Women and children also came and pleaded that he would save them from the violence of a sack, until at last the grim old veteran, hero of a hundred battles, gave way.

"I had rather be carried to my grave," he said, but he ordered the white flag raised on the fort.

And thus peaceably fell New Amsterdam in the year of our Lord 1664.

The articles of capitulation were agreed on next morning. They provided that free intercourse with Holland was to continue, that citizens of every race and creed were to be secured in person, property, customs, and religion. Stuyvesant and his men were to march out with drums beating, colors flying, and matchlocks lighted, and embark on the vessel which was to bear them to the fatherland.

This program was fully carried out on the 8th of September, 1664. As the Dutch marched out the English entered, and raised their red cross flag over the fort and public buildings. Nicolls was proclaimed governor, the fort rechristened James, in honor of the duke, and the province named New York for the same reason.

The United Provinces exclaimed loudly against the injustice of the conquest, and waged a long and bloody war with England because of it. Stuyvesant, too, was blamed for yielding up the fort, but hurried to Amsterdam and made a strong defense. Afterwards, his family, his property, and friends being in New York, he returned, and lived many years in his fine old country-house, which stood near the corner of what is now Third Avenue and Twelfth Street. There he died in 1672, one of the heroic figures of his age. His house, garden, and bouwery continued to be for many years one of the landmarks of the city. The house was of wood, two stories high, with projecting story, and stood about one hundred and fifty feet east of Third Avenue and forty feet north of Twelfth Street. In front of it was the garden, laid out in quaint old Dutch style with formal paths and flower beds describing almost every geometrical figure. In this garden, near the house, Stuyvesant planted a pear tree, which for more than two hundred years kept his memory green and indicated to passers-by the site of his dwelling. Generation after generation of his descendants grew up and passed away. Year by year the city crept steadily northward, invaded his farm, and caused streets to be laid out through his garden; then the old pear tree, still green, vigorous, and fruitful, found itself at the corner of Third Avenue and Thirteenth

Stuyvesant's Pear Tree.

Street. Then careful hands placed an iron railing about it to protect it. At last, after it had stood on the corner for sixty years, it was blown down in a great storm in February, 1867, and the last memento of the lion-hearted governor ceased to exist.

His widow, Judith Bayard, lived on in the old mansion until her death in 1687, and founded by will the present Saint Mark's Church, which stands on a part of the Stuyvesant farm, and in which the ashes of the governor rest.

## VI. DUTCH MANNERS AND CUSTOMS.

IF in the preceding pages we have spoken little of the life of the people, it was from our desire to present a clear and connected idea of the founding of our noble city and of the causes which led up to it, and not because we deemed such details trivial or unimportant.

For a generation the life of the pioneers was rude and hard. They dwelt at first in tents and dugouts, later in small, one-room cabins with thatched straw roofs and chimneys of small, square sticks mortared with mud. There was much hard and rude work to be done; forests were to be cleared, lands drained, plowed, and sowed, quarries opened, a fort, brickkilns, houses, flouring mills, and sawmills built, and streets and roads laid out and paved.

By 1664, however, New Amsterdam had become a city with not a few of the amenities and refinements of civilized life. Let us imagine that we stroll through it some beautiful June morning in 1664, and look upon the burghers at their work and play.

We might have come over from Brooklyn by the rowboat ferry which then landed near the present Peck Slip. As we stepped ashore we should have seen both cleared fields and forests about us. Though the "fferry road" wound south, following the present line of Pearl

Street, which then ran along the pebbly beach of the East
River, the streets now lying between—Water, South,
and Front—were then crossed by the tide. At what is
now Maiden Lane we should have come upon a foot-
path which here crossed our road, coming down to the
river from Broadway, and skirting the shores of several
clear-water ponds fed by springs, their combined outlet
being a little brook that came leaping gayly down to join
the river; and here a pretty scene would have presented
itself. A bevy of beautiful maidens, with bare, dimpled
arms, are wetting linen in the basins, and spreading it
in the sun on the verdant slope of the hill to the west,
chatting volubly the while in their musical tongue.
Their own fingers have spun the linen from the flax and
woven it in the loom, and now they are spreading it in
the sun to bleach. They and their mothers before them
formed the path,
hence called Maagde
Paatje ("Maidens'
Path"), which the
English changed to
our present Maiden
Lane.

Pleased and inter-
ested, we should have
journeyed on, and at
the present line of

The Wall. 1664.

Wall Street would have been stopped abruptly by a
blank wall of palisades—great timbers twelve feet high,
set three feet deep in the earth, with stout posts at every
rod, rising two feet above the palisades, to which split

rails were nailed, thus forming a fence two feet above the tops of the palisades. Before us would have been an arched gateway, the key of the arch being carved with strange-looking figures and crowned with a cupola and gilded weathercock. Let us imagine that the great nail-studded oaken gate is open, and we enter. Once within, we examine the wall more closely. At the water's edge on the east is a square blockhouse with holes between the timbers for muskets, and a "half-moon" or semicircular battery projecting into the water and mounting two cannon, one pointing up the river, the other down.

Foot of Wall Street, 1674.

There is a guard here, a single soldier in loose gray blouse and baggy breeches, with an ancient flintlock musket thrown over his shoulder. These blockhouses are placed at intervals along the wall quite over to the Hudson, while at Broadway there is another gate and arched gateway. Without is a chevaux-de-frise of stumps with their fanglike roots upturned, and within a broad ditch and a sod rampart.

The guard at the gate tells us that the wall is 2,340 feet long, that it cost 3,166 guilders, and was built in 1653, when the people feared a descent from the English and hostile Indians on the north. Thanking the sentry, we are about to continue, when we are beset by a half score of ragged, sooty urchins with their cry of "Sweep ho!" There is a wide lane flanking the wall (hence called Wall Street), and on its inner side is a row of rude thatched cabins, the Five Points of New Amsterdam, abodes of boatmen, sweeps, tapsters, and social outcasts.

We will walk slowly along the water front, staring at everything, as might be expected of curious travelers from a far country. Here are queer, half-moon docks with no vessels moored to them, but instead placid and substantial-looking burghers, talking, smoking, or watching fish lines thrown from the dock. Their stores and dwellings are across the street, quaint, peaked-roofed buildings with crowstep gables, store beneath and dwelling above, and, overtopping all, the great stone Stadt Huys, or City Hall, with its gallows in front. The busiest place of all is the city dock, the first built on Manhattan Island, precursor of the thirty miles or more of busy wharves of the modern city. The merchants call it the "Hooft," and the water in front the "Road-

City Hall and Great Dock, 1679.

stead." There are scows, skiffs, periaguas, and canoes moored to it, but no large craft; they must anchor in the Roadstead, being forbidden to come alongside, in order to prevent smuggling, and also to keep the sailors from roaming through the city.

A fleet of scows and small boats is employed removing cargo to the dock from the ships of all descriptions anchored in the Roadstead. These are laden with divers articles, according to the port from which they sailed. Thus, a "Holland ship," as those from the mother country are called, has dry goods, wet goods, hardware, and perhaps a few of those "cow calves" and "ewe milk sheep" mentioned by the old chroniclers as being staple articles of export to New Netherlands during this period. One of the scows is laden with dried fish and English goods from a "snow" just arrived from Boston; a second with hogsheads of tobacco from a Virginia "ketch;" a third with savage, unkempt negroes from the west coast of Africa, on their way from the slaver *White Horse*, to be sold in the slave market at public auction to the highest bidder.

Leister's House.

A galley from Curaçao is unloading costly dyewoods and tropical fruits into a fourth, while a fifth, tied to a "pincke" from Barbados, is receiving barrels of sugar and hogsheads of molasses, the latter exuding sweetness in the hot sun. Molasses smears the deck of the scow and now and then causes a fall among the barefooted slaves that man her. On the other hand, this sloop of the great patroon of Rensselaerwyck is sending ashore bales of costly furs—mink, otter, beaver, wolf, bear, and others. All must be landed at the city dock and pay duty; consequently the latter is a busy place, as before remarked. Gangs of Angola slaves receive the goods, and after they are duly entered trundle them off across the street to the merchants' warehouses, or to the company's five great stone storehouses that stand in a row between what will be Bridge and Stone streets later.

The four great merchants of New Amsterdam at this period—Cornelis Steenwyck, Pieter Cornelissen Vanderveen, Govert Loockermans, and Isaac Allerton—are among them in their cloth coats with silver buttons and baggy breeches, to see that they get good weight and measure, and that the negroes keep to their task and practice no thievery; indeed, Cornelis Steenwyck is so

East River near Coenties Slip, 1658.

careful that he is followed by a negro woman with needle and thread, who sews up any rents in bags or bales that his sharp eyes detect.

Turning again to the water front, we find a warning placard off the future Coenties Slip forbidding vessels of fifty tons or under to anchor between there and the fort under a heavy penalty. There is another near the future Fulton Street forbidding any vessel at all to moor above that point, thus collecting all the craft in the harbor into one locality. Quite a fleet there is, too, and such queer craft, with their square bows, broad beams, and sterns built so high you would think the first gale from astern would catch them up and bury them fathoms deep by the bows—very different from the craft of grace and beauty that later gathered at these wharves. Their names are quite as quaint and curious—*Flower of Guilder, Sea Mew, Little Fox, Blue Cock, New Netherlands Fortune, Little Crane, Great Christopher, New Netherland Indian*, and so on.

We are about to proceed, following the ferry road on to the fort, when we notice a stir on the dock, and looking up, see that the flag on the flagstaff has been hoisted to the masthead, which means that a Holland ship is standing in. Such an event will be too common for notice in later days, but to these good people it means tidings from home and kin, of fathers and mothers, brothers and sisters, wives and sweethearts; news of the world, also, up to the vessel's sailing eight weeks before, and to the merchants news of ventures, fate of argosies.

So they hasten to the Battery and welcome the new-comer with waving of hats and handkerchiefs. By and by a gun from the fort brings the vessel to off the Battery. The haven master boards her, inspects papers and manifests, and she is then allowed to proceed to her anchorage in the Roadstead, and to discharge her passengers.

At Bridge Street is a great bridge over the Heere Graft, or Principal Canal, which here enters from the East River, and extends along the line of Broad Street up to Exchange Place. No doubt the burghers built it

Canal and Bridge in Broad Street.

to remind them of Holland. They cherish it highly and take the utmost care of it. Its sides are protected by wooden piling. No one may throw refuse into it or defile its waters. There are broad sidewalks on either side of it, patrolled by a burly "Graft officer," whose duty it is to keep the siding in repair, prevent nuisances, and "lay the boats, canoes, and other craft that come therein in order."

There are many of the latter within it now—Long Island farmers laden with produce, Indians in canoes with furs and game to sell. The bridge near its mouth is a famous meeting place for the merchants, the first Merchants' Exchange; at its mouth are the company's stores before mentioned, and opposite it the Roadstead.

Let us next turn into Whitehall Street, which will lead us to the fort. It is well built up on one side with solid stone and brick houses showing checkerwork

The Fort.

fronts and crowstep gables, and overlooking the Battery and the shining reaches of the bay. It is quite the patrician quarter. Here at the foot is Governor Stuyvesant's town mansion, known far and wide as the "White Hall," and giving the street its name. Behind each house is a garden gay with flowers, the wonderful tulip of Holland predominating, and in the rear of this an orchard of pear, peach, plum, apple, quince, and apricot trees well loaded with young fruit. Primeval oaks and elms spared from the ancient forests shade this really beautiful thoroughfare.

It leads us up to the Bowling Green, or "Common," the first laid out by the city fathers. Whitehall Street enters this from the east, while Broadway leaves it on the north. On the south or seaward side stands the fort, a quadrangular earthwork having bastions faced with stone, and mounting twenty-two curious, wide-mouthed brass and bronze cannon. Bombards, serpentines, culverins, and so on, the soldiers call them, and they throw stone as well as iron balls.

The interior, or parade, is one hundred and fifty feet square, and in its center is planted the tall flagstaff we saw from the water front; and there proudly floats the white, blue, and orange flag of the West India Company. A quaint windmill, its tower turning on a pivot, stands on the northwest bastion, whence come the prevailing winds.

The principal object within the fort, however, is the great stone church built by Kieft in 1642, with its two peaked roofs, and the tower looming aloft between. The government house, a plain brick structure, also built by Kieft, stands beside it, and with the jail, barracks, and storehouses of stone completes the list of buildings within the fort.

There are many soldiers lounging about, while little groups of townspeople and sightseers promenade the ramparts, for the fort is one of the lions of the infant city.

A little wearied with our sightseeing, we will now cross the Green to the tavern of the worshipful Marten Cregier, president of the burgomasters and captain of the burgher guard, which tavern is the fashionable inn of the city. Whenever the governors of the neighboring colonies, titled visitors from abroad, military and naval officers, book-making travelers, and commissioners sent to treat on vexed questions of boundaries or runaway slaves or illicit trade, come to town, they are at once referred to the inn of the good burgomaster.

Scarcely have we drawn rein when the host appears to welcome us, and a hostler holds the stirrup while we dismount. Crossing the broad, brick-floored stoop, or porch, furnished with comfortable wooden benches, we pass through the two-leaved oaken door into the wide hall, on one side of which is the parlor, with oiled floor and ponderous stiff-backed Dutch furniture, and on the other the great public room of the inn. The floor of the latter has been freshly sprinkled with clean white sand brought from Coney Island by the "vlie boats," and it has been drawn into whorls and grotesque figures by Gretchen's tireless broom. The walls are graced by deers' antlers, on which hang the long "goose guns" of the landlord and his guests, by placards, and by funny Dutch prints of hunting scenes and the like. In one corner is a sideboard, rich with decanters, bottles, and glasses, and a rack stuck full of long pipes, each inscribed with the name of its owner; for the inn is the resort of the better class of citizens, the merchants and gentry, filling the place of the modern clubhouse and exchange. Two very fat merchants are already here, seated at a little table, sipping foaming Sopus beer, smoking contentedly, and now and then venturing a remark. The placards give us a vivid idea of the iron rule of Stuyvesant, for most of them are ordinances telling what the tapsters and the people may not do. One commands the innkeeper not to give or sell any strong drink to the Indians; another commands him to report at once to the proper officer any one hurt or wounded in his house; another forbids him to admit or entertain any company in the evening after the ringing of the farmers' bell, or sell or furnish any liquors on the Sabbath, " travelers and boarders alone excepted, before three o'clock in the afternoon, when divine service is finished."

Does it not seem strange to read the following placard? " Whereas we are informed of the great ravages the wolf commits on the small cattle, therefore, to animate and encourage the proprietors who will go out and shoot the same, we have resolved to authorize the assistant schout [sheriff] and schepens to give public notice that whoever shall exhibit a wolf to them which hath been shot on this island on this side Harlem shall be promptly paid therefor by them, for a wolf fl. 20, and for a she-wolf fl. 30, in wampum or the value thereof." The thickets that cover the greater portion of the island are favorite retreats for these and other wild beasts.

After a substantial Dutch supper of wild fowl and game, we sit with the other guests on the stoop, where Phyllis, the barmaid, brings us spiced sangaree and pipes. The sun is sinking behind the noble forest that still lines Broadway on the west, and the people seek their stoops to enjoy the evening hour. Nearly all these have their burden of beautiful women and staid, taciturn men, the former chatting among themselves or with acquaintances, who, strolling by, stop for neighborly gossip.

As strangers we are interested in the scene that

A Tea Party.

gradually unfolds before us. Carriages filled with ladies and gentlemen roll by, and among them the governor's state coach, with the ladies of his family bowing and smiling. From the fort comes the measured tread of the sentinel. Lovers stroll by arm in arm on their way to the Bowling Green, the maidens of a beauty so marked that English travelers will note the fact in their books.

Nor are the common people wanting. There are laborers and artisans in toil-stained frocks and leather breeches, bare-armed servant girls in homespun waists and short gowns, turbaned negresses bringing "tea water" from the pump. Soon Gabriel Carpesey, the town herdsman, appears driving in the flocks for the evening milking from the common lands (at the present City Hall Park), where he drove them to pasture in the morning. At every gate he stops and blows his horn to tell the householder that his cow has come home.

By and by a little stir up the street attracts our attention, and looking up, there comes in view a hunting party of Indians, each warrior placing his foot in the footprint of the one preceding him, and gazing neither left nor right. They bear to market haunches of venison, wild turkeys, and the quarters of an elk. What a motley array! For instance, one sports a doublet of bearskin, another is clad in a blanket only, a third stalks along in a coat of raccoon skins, while a fourth is clad in a mantle made of the brilliant-hued feathers of the wild turkey.

The sight leads a stout burgher at our side to say: "Never was a people better fed. The woods swarm with game,—elk, deer, bear, hare, turkeys, partridges, quail,—and the waters with ducks, geese, and swans. An Indian will sell a buck for five guilders. The worshipful patroon De Vries once shot a wild turkey that weighed thirty pounds. Hendrik de Backer killed once eleven wild geese at one shot of his big goose gun. As to fish, we have sturgeon, salmon, bass, drum, shad, cod, smelts, sheepshead, herring, mackerel, blackfish, lobster, weakfish, oysters, clams, and scallops."

Scarcely have the Indians passed when a bell in the fort tolls heavily,—one, two, three, up to nine,—and with its last note the city gates close with a clang. It is the curfew bell—the "farmers' bell," the people call it, perhaps because after it egress to the farms without is shut off by the closing of the gates.

As its last melodious notes sink into the evening air, the lights in stores and houses fade, the streets cease to echo with footsteps, and New Amsterdam sinks into slumber.

At the first stroke of the bell comely Gretchen comes to show us to our chamber. It is a large, square room overhead, with a half-dozen bunks or berths set into the partition wall, and closed by a sort of trapdoor that lets down on hinges. She puts the tallow candle on the mantel and departs. We prepare for rest and then inspect our quarters. There are two feather beds in each bunk, a large and a small one. We jump in and pull the smaller one over us for a cover. By and by Gretchen returns, closes the trapdoor, and removes the candle, leaving us to sleep peacefully in our box. Next morning we rise early and go for a stroll on the Green. It is much larger than the Green of the modern city, with finer shade, and as we enter it we meet scores of little black boys, turbaned Phyllises, and stout peasant maids rosy of cheek, bareheaded and bare-armed, bringing water from the town pump over there against the fort wall.

As it happens, next day is Sunday, and, with all

A Wedding in New Amsterdam.

respectable New Amsterdam, we go to church, hoping to see more of the people and their ways. The church is in the fort, and we are there at the first stroke of the bell, being rewarded therefor by seeing the worshipers pass in review before us. There are two great columns that converge at the fort gate, one coming down Broadway, the other up Whitehall Street and the ferry road, while the Green rapidly fills with the wagons and carts of the country people who have come from the bouweries in the upper part of the island and on the Long Island shore.

They make a gallant show, this company of church-goers, for great attention is paid to dress, at least by gentlemen, and the wealthy Englishmen and French Huguenots who have settled in New Amsterdam during the past twenty years have introduced rich and splendid costumes.

The ladies wear on their heads colored hoods of silk or taffeta instead of bonnets; their hair is curled and frizzled, and sprinkled with powder; on their fingers are gold and diamond rings, golden lockets on their bosoms, and attached to their girdles by fine gold chains are their Bibles and psalm books, richly bound in gold and silver. From beneath their quilted petticoats their feet, in low shoes and colored hose, " like little mice steal in and out." The petticoat is the most important article of feminine attire at this period. The rich gown is cut away in front to display it; in material it may be of cloth, silk, satin, camlet, or grosgrain, and of colors to please the fancy of the wearer, red, blue, black, white, and purple predominating.

The gentlemen display the latest London or Amsterdam fashions. Their heads are covered with powdered, full-bottomed wigs, and the wide brims of their soft hats are looped up on the sides with rosettes. Their long coats have two rows of silver buttons in front, and the wide pockets are trimmed with silver lace; the material is colored stuff and black velvet and broadcloth. Their waistcoats, or doublets, are of bright-colored cloth or velvet, and embroidered with silver lace. Their breeches, generally of velvet, end at the knee in black silk stockings, and they wear on their feet low shoes adorned with large silver buckles. These are the gentry, of course, but the commonalty are well represented —honest Hans in loose blouse and baggy breeches of homespun, Katrina in linsey-woolsey gown and petticoat, with deep poke bonnet on her head.

The worshipers have nearly all entered when the carriage of Governor Stuyvesant, with its blazoned panels, dashes up, and the governor and his family alight—the governor, his wife, and his widowed sister, Mrs. Bayard. The former bears himself like a soldier in spite of the wooden leg, bound with bands of silver, which replaces the one lost in honorable fight with the Spanish at Saint Martin. Mrs. Stuyvesant, a beautiful French lady, daughter of a Huguenot clergyman of Paris, is famed for her beauty and her elegant toilets.

Let us follow this stately party into the church. It is a plain, bare interior, with a very high pulpit, and over it a sounding board like a bird with wings outspread.

Scarcely are we seated ere the burgomasters and schepens in their black official robes enter from the vestry, preceded by the "koeck," or bell ringer, bearing the cushion for the official pew, and followed by good

Domine Megapolensis, also in black robes. At the foot of the pulpit stairs he pauses and utters a silent prayer, while the people bow their heads. As he takes his seat in the pulpit, the zeikentrooster, or lay reader, rises and reads the morning lesson.

The orderly and decorous service proceeds. When the sands have all run out of the hourglass before him, the zeikentrooster announces the fact by three taps of his cane, and the domine brings his sermon to a close. Then the koeck inserts the public notices to be read in the end of his wand of office, and hands them up to the preacher. This being done, the elders rise in their pews, while the minister delivers a homily on the duty of remembering the poor, after which the elders pass through the church, and receive in a little black bag fastened to a long pole the alms of the worshipers.

Service over, the people proceed to their homes, and the poor schout-fiscal is relieved of his task of patrolling the streets, seeing that no taprooms are open, and no Indians or negro slaves gaming; for although Sunday afternoon is a holiday for the latter, an ordinance sternly forbids their playing or gaming "during the hours of morning service."

With the afternoon before us, we can follow one of the wagons which has come down from the Walloon village on the Brooklyn shore.

The wagon with the farmer and his stout, rosy-cheeked vrouw passes out the water gate by which we entered, and so along the woodsy road to the ferry house. The latter is merely an open shed roofed with thatch and extending into the water, so that the flatboat and two or three skiffs that comprise the ferry fleet may be moored to it. Cornelis Dircksen and his strong-armed lads are at hand, since it is Sunday; had it been a week day we should have to take the long horn that hangs on

Ferry to Brooklyn.

yonder tree and blow a blast as loud as Roderick Dhu's in order to summon them from their work in the fields.

The ferry ordinances are posted in the house, together with the tariff of fares—a two-horse wagon or cart with the horses, 2 florins[1] 10 stivers; a one-horse wagon, 2 florins; for every man, woman, Indian, or squaw, 6 stivers, but if there are more than one in the party 3 stivers each; children under ten years of age half fare; one horse or horned beast, 1 florin 10 stivers; a hogshead of tobacco 16 stivers, a tun of beer the same, and smaller articles in proportion. One rule stipulates that the ferryman shall be bound to ferry over passengers from

[1] A florin is forty cents American money, a stiver one cent.

five in the morning until eight at night, " provided the windmill hath not taken in its sail."

The tide is ebbing swiftly toward Governors Island, and as the wind blows stiffly against it there is an ugly sea. Consequently the unwieldy boat is borne steadily toward the island, dancing and bobbing on the choppy waves, and we begin to fear that we shall be wrecked on its rocky shores, when the men succeed in getting her into the slack water on the Brooklyn side. Then comes the long pull up to the ferry landing at the foot of the later Fulton Street. We sympathize with Cornelis when he mops his heated brow and remarks that it is " a long pull and little money." The boat has been an hour in crossing.

There is a ferry house here also, a tavern, and a few small dwellings of laborers and workmen. The road runs diagonally up the Heights and on, passing scarcely a house on the way, until it reaches Flatbush, some five miles distant, where there is a considerable settlement. At the Wallabout (later the Navy Yard) the Walloons have a pretty village; but the modern patrician quarter, the Heights, is crowned with nature's temple, the primeval forest, as is almost the entire site of the modern city.

After a pleasant visit we return from Brooklyn and ride out by the Broad Way, or " land gate." The famous thoroughfare was first laid out as a cow path from the fort to the common pasture lands. Now it is lined with residences as far as the gate, and above that winds as a country road as far as the site of the modern City Hall, where it ends in primeval forest. The Dutch first called it Heere Straat (Principal Street), later Breede Wig, which the English translated Broadway. Just without the gate is the West India Company's garden, afterwards the site of Trinity churchyard. Next above is the farm of Jan Jansen Damen, and next to that the company's farm, which later will be confiscated by the English, who will call it the "King's Farm" and grant it to Trinity Church. This farm lies between the modern Fulton and Chambers streets. Above this lies a rough tract of sixty-two acres, owned by Annetje Jans, the widow of Domine Bogardus. It will be sold in 1670 by a part of her heirs to Governor Lovelace, and he not being able to pay for it, it will be seized by his successor, Governor Andros, and known as the "Duke's Farm," and later granted to Trinity Church by Queen Anne.

At this time (1664) New Amsterdam contains two hundred and twenty houses and fourteen hundred people.

## VII. THE ENGLISH COLONIAL PERIOD.

WE return now to take up the thread of later history. Henceforth for one hundred and eleven years, except for a brief period, New York was to remain a British colony. It must be admitted that the change was a beneficial one. Instead of a mere trading post, governed by a commercial monopoly and surrounded by hostile colonies, she now became one of several provinces under the same government, speaking the same tongue, and having the same general interests. She did not achieve full liberty, but she had *more* liberty. In treating of this period we shall have space for only the more important events, and shall give due prominence to the one great principle which underlay the rest—the struggle of the people for their rights, and especially for the right to govern themselves.

Twenty royal governors ruled New York during this period, under eight kings and queens—Charles II. and James II. of the Stuart line, William and Mary of the house of Orange, Queen Anne of the Stuart line again, and lastly the Georges I., II., and III. of the Brunswick line.[1] As a rule the royal governors were not noted for

[1] The names of these governors, with their terms of office, were: Richard Nicolls, 1664–1668; Francis Lovelace, 1668–1673; Sir Edmund Andros, 1674–1682; Thomas Dongan, 1683–1689; Henry Sloughter,

patriotism or statesmanship. A few were men of sagacity and experience in public affairs, who were appointed because of their fitness. Colonel Nicolls, the first, was one of the most capable. Certain problems and difficulties confronted him that were not met with by his successors. A conquered people was to be placated, new conditions were to be established, special laws provided. Nicolls performed the task with tact and discretion. The Dutch were secured in their homes, business, and religion, and for nearly a year were left in possession of their city government. Then, when their fear and suspicion of the English had been greatly allayed, the latter was changed to the English form; schout, burgomasters, and schepens giving place to mayor, aldermen, and councilors.

A code of laws was framed called the "Duke's Laws," more liberal in many respects than those of the Dutch. Trial by jury was established, a court of sessions also for the city, and a justice court for each town, with the right of appeal to the higher court. Treason, murder, kidnaping, striking parents, denying the true God, and some other crimes were punishable by death. Slavery was permitted, but no Christians were to be enslaved

1691 (died July 23, 1691); Benjamin Fletcher, 1692–1698; Earl of Bellomont, 1698 (died March 5, 1701); Lord Cornbury, 1702–1708; Lord Lovelace, 1708 (died May 6, 1709); Robert Hunter, 1710–1719; William Burnet, 1720–1728; Lord John Montgomery, 1728 (died July 1, 1731); William Cosby, 1732 (died March 10, 1736); George Clinton, 1743–1753; Sir Danvers Osborne, 1753 (died October 12, 1753); Sir Charles Hardy, 1755–1757; Robert Monckton, 1761–1765; Sir Henry Moore, 1765–1770; Earl of Dunmore, 1770; Sir William Tryon, 1771 (deposed in the Revolution). The interregnums between some of these dates were filled by lieutenant governors or provisional governors.

except criminals sentenced by lawful authority. In order to trade with the Indians merchants must procure a license. No Indian was allowed to powwow, or perform incantations to the devil. No sect was to be favored above another, and no Christian was to be molested for his religious opinions. The patents of the great patroons were confirmed to them under the English titles of "manors." The Dutch were secured in their ownership of the great stone church in the fort, and worshiped there in the morning, yielding it to the English congregation in the afternoon.

During the war of England against the Netherlands and France (1665-1667), New York was in constant apprehension of an attack from the Dutch fleet, but escaped for the time. In the second war of England against the Netherlands (1672-1674), in which the former had France for an ally, New York was not so fortunate. In the spring of 1673 the Dutch dispatched a squadron under command of two brave admirals, Evertsen and Binckes, to recover their lost territory in America, and to inflict as much damage as possible on English commerce in those seas.

On the 29th of June the sentinel on Fort James (as Fort Amsterdam had been named) saw this fleet enter and cast anchor in the lower bay, with some twenty English prizes in tow.

Governor Lovelace, who had succeeded Nicolls in 1668, was in Hartford consulting with Governor Winthrop of Connecticut concerning the defense of the two colonies, and a messenger was at once sent posthaste for him, while Captain Manning, in command of Fort James, charged his guns, and sent his drummers out to beat the alarm. The Dutch admirals, however, were as sensible of the value of time as Nicolls had been in 1664. They forthwith moved their fleet to within a musket shot of the fort, and sent Manning a laconic summons to surrender. "We have come for our own," they added grimly, "and our own we will have." Manning sought to gain time by asking for terms, but Evertsen replied that he had already promised protection to life and property, and that if the Dutch flag was not hoisted over the fort in half an hour he should fire on it; "and the glass is already turned up," he added significantly.

But Manning refused to surrender, and when the half hour had expired the fleet fired a broadside into the fort, killing several and wounding more. At the same time a detachment of six hundred Dutch landed at a point behind the present Trinity Church, and assailed the garrison in the rear. Manning, finding the odds too great, surrendered, and was allowed to march out with the honors of war, drums beating and colors flying; while the dragon flag fluttered down from the fort, and the blue, white, and orange was again triumphantly raised over it. A second time the fort was renamed, this time William Hendrik, and the province called New Orange, both after William, Prince of Orange, the pride and hope of the Dutch state.

But the city did not long remain in possession of the Dutch, for in the treaty of Westminster (1674) they relinquished forever all claims to their former territory of New Netherlands. Lovelace did not return as governor, however, Sir Edmund Andros, a member of King

Charles's household and bailiff of Guernsey, having been appointed in his place. The principal event of Andros's reign was the granting to New York by James of a provincial assembly.

The people quickly found that, although their condition was more tolerable than under Stuyvesant, they were still ruled by one man, the Duke of York, three thousand miles away. They desired a voice in the management of their own affairs, as had the colonies to the east and south of them; and in the summer of 1681 they sent to the duke a petition signed by many thousand citizens, praying that he would henceforth govern them by means of a council, assembly, and governor, as was done by the king in his colonies.

James carefully considered the matter, and on being advised that in order to collect a revenue it would be necessary to give the province an assembly, granted the prayer of the petitioners. But as Andros by his haughty manner and tyrannical acts had become obnoxious to the people, he decided to recall him and appoint Thomas Dongan, a tried soldier, who as lieutenant governor of Tangier in Africa had had experience in governing. Dongan reached the city in August, 1683, and one of his first official acts was to issue writs for deputies to the first Provincial Assembly of New York, who were to be elected by the people.

From these ancient writs we learn that New York's bounds then extended east as far as the Connecticut River, and included the islands of Nantucket, Marthas Vineyard, and Long Island. The districts that returned deputies to this first assembly were New York, Albany,

Rensselaerwyck, Esopus on the Hudson, Long Island, Staten Island, Pemaquid, and Marthas Vineyard, the whole number of members being eighteen, most of them Dutch in nationality. This first assembly of New York convened on October 17, 1683, with Matthias Nicolls as speaker, and sat for three weeks. Its first act was to accept a " Charter of Liberties and Privileges," which had been granted by the duke. This instrument provided for self-government, self-taxation, and freedom of conscience, three principles which the people had long been striving for. Another act levied a duty on goods imported. A third created four courts of justice—a town court, a county court, a general court of oyer and terminer, and a supreme court, the latter composed of the governor and council; even from the latter court an appeal might be had to the king. This assembly also passed a naturalization act by which all residents of the colony except slaves might become citizens by professing Christianity and taking the oath of allegiance to the king.

But before King Charles could sign this charter, and thereby make it a law, he died (February 6, 1685), and James ascended the throne. Now that their patron and proprietor was on the throne the people looked for even greater favors; but alas! they soon found that James the king was a very different person from James the duke. As king he discovered that the Charter of Liberties and Privileges was too liberal, and refused to confirm it, although he allowed the colonists to enjoy its provisions during his pleasure. However, this made very little difference, for in November, 1688, the Dutch prince, William of Orange, who had married James's daughter Mary, landed in England and raised the standard of revolt, whereupon James abdicated in favor of his son-in-law and daughter. You can learn all about the causes of this revolt, which makes an interesting story, in your Macaulay or Green.

Before his abdication, however, James had matured a plot against his American colonies in the north that was intended to deprive them of their long-cherished liberties. He issued a decree in the spring of 1688 uniting all the colonies north of the fortieth parallel in one great province, to be called New England. It included New Jersey, New York, and the New England colonies, Pennsylvania being excepted. Sir Edmund Andros, whom the colonists already disliked, was named governor of the united province, with headquarters at Boston, and arrived in New York in August, 1688, to receive the submission of the people. He came in state, accompanied by a large and imposing retinue. The City Guard, a regiment of foot and a troop of horse, in shining regimentals, received him and escorted him to Fort James, where his commission was read to the assembled people; later it was read in the City Hall to a more select audience. The seal of New York was brought into the governor's presence, and broken and defaced by order of the king, and the great seal of New England was adopted in its place.

These things related more to the province, however, than to the city. One thing James did for the latter during his brief reign for which we should hold him in grateful remembrance: he gave her the Great Charter, on which, as on a firm foundation, the subsequent charters of 1708 and 1730 were based. This instrument confirmed all previous " rights and privileges " granted the city, and gave it in addition the City Hall, the great dock and bridge (probably the bridge over the canal in Broad Street), the two market houses, the ferry, and the vacant, unpatented shore lands above low-water mark. Most of these vested rights we still enjoy, and they are yielding the city large revenues to-day, mostly in docks and ferries.

The people of New England especially were very much incensed against King James for thus depriving them of their chartered rights, as well as against Andros, his agent, and the moment that news of the former's abdication reached Boston her citizens seized Andros and thrust him into prison.

## VIII. THE ENGLISH COLONIAL PERIOD
(*Continued*)—LEISLER'S REVOLT.

A CHAOTIC condition of affairs arose in New York as the result of the abdication of James and the imprisonment of Andros. Two factions at once appeared, composed, as to race, of the English against the Dutch; as to class, of the aristocrats against the commoners; as to religion, of the Church of England against the Dutch Reformed Church.

The strife was as to who should rule the city. The English held that the officers appointed by James then in power should stand until their successors should be appointed by William and Mary, in which position they had law and precedent on their side. The Dutch party held that with the flight of James his authority ceased in the colonies as much as in England, and that therefore the people under their charter should appoint officers to rule until the pleasure of William should be known. Lieutenant Governor Nicholson and the three members of Governor Andros's council, Frederick Phillipse, Mayor Stephanus Van Cortlandt, and Nicholas Bayard, were the leaders of the English party. Phillipse was lord of the manor of Phillipseborough; his old manor house you may still see in the heart of the city of Yonkers, in use as the city hall. Van Cortlandt was mayor, and had been judge of the admiralty. Bayard

Phillipse Manor House (now City Hall), Yonkers.

was a connection of Stuyvesant, had been mayor of the city, and was now colonel of the regiment of city militia.

The leaders of the democratic party were Jacob Leisler and Jacob Millborne. Leisler was German born, but had lived in New York some thirty years. He was a prosperous merchant, a deacon in the Dutch Reformed Church, captain of one of the six train bands which made up Colonel Bayard's regiment of militia, a man of much energy and force of character, but uneducated, self-willed, passionate, and unbalanced in judgment; a fanatic on the subject of popery, a stern hater of the English, their church, and their institutions. Millborne was Leisler's son-in-law, a man of better education, but of far less principle.

The struggle for power began on April 29, 1689, by Leisler's refusing to pay the duties on a cargo of wine he had imported, "because," he said, "Collector Ploughman was a papist, and therefore not qualified to perform his duties under the Protestant sovereigns William and Mary."

A long discussion in the City Hall between the council and Leisler was ended by the latter's declaring that he would never pay a penny to Ploughman. And now strange rumors began to be whispered about the town by the ignorant burghers. It was said that Lieutenant Governor Nicholson was plotting to betray the city to the French. His papist emissaries filled the woods on Staten Island, and met him nightly in consultation. King James, who had fled to France, was on the seas with a French fleet, to whom Nicholson would deliver up the city. The chief Dutch citizens had already been won over to popery. Ex-Governor Dongan, who still lingered in New York, had formed a plot to murder the Protestants and yield the city to the Catholics. These and many other disquieting rumors flew about. This fear and unrest of the public mind must be considered in order to understand what followed.

A very little thing at last brought on the conflict. Nicholson resided in the governor's house in the fort, and coming in late one night found a member of the militia company which had been detailed to guard the fort standing sentinel at the gate. This was contrary to regulations, and calling the sergeant in command, he reprimanded him. The latter replied that Lieutenant Cuyler had ordered it, and that officer in turn laid the blame on his superior officer, Captain de Peyster. Nicholson, who distrusted the militia, fell into a passion at this, and said he would rather see the town in flames than be spied upon and overruled by his militia captains. This was at once tortured into a threat to burn the city, and soon the rumor flew about that the governor had formed a plot to fire the city and murder all the Dutch citizens the next Sunday as they came to church in the fort. The six train bands which formed the city militia were nearly all Dutch, and, led by Leisler, they now determined, in order to save their lives and property, to seize the fort and government.

The Sunday came,—May 31, 1689,—and at noon a single drumbeat was heard. Captain Leisler's company at once mustered before his house, and was led by Sergeant Stoll to the fort, where Lieutenant Cuyler, who was in charge, admitted them. In a few moments Leisler appeared and took command. On hearing of this, Colonel Bayard, commander of the militia, went to the fort and ordered the soldiers to disperse; but Stoll coolly told him that they disowned all authority of the Andros government. Having no force to defend himself, Lieutenant Governor Nicholson made no resistance, and shortly after sailed for England to lay the matter before King William, leaving affairs in the hands of his three councilors.

Leisler, by virtue of his command over the City Guard, now ruled as governor of the city. His first act was to write an address to William and Mary in behalf of "the militia and inhabitants of New York," describing the revolution and its causes, and pledging to them the loyal support of himself and those acting with him. At first he governed with justice and moderation, but he seems soon to have become intoxicated with the possession of unlimited power, and treated those opposed to him with great arrogance and even cruelty. About the middle of June two envoys came from Hartford bearing orders to proclaim William and Mary in New York, as they had shortly before been proclaimed in Boston and Hartford. The envoys also bore a royal proclamation confirming all Protestant officers in the colonies in their places. This was fatal to the claims of Leisler and his party, and spurred them on to the rash and fatal extremity of resistance. Mayor Van Cortlandt rode far up into Westchester to intercept the envoys, but Leisler managed to secure both proclamations from them, and read the first named in the fort on the 22d, although Mayor Van Cortlandt demanded that they should be delivered to him as the lawful authority. Two days later the mayor succeeded in securing a copy of the second proclamation, which constituted himself and his colleagues, Phillipse and Bayard, the only legal government, since they were Protestants and had received their commissions from the crown. The three met with the common council to consult on the best plan of regaining their authority without provoking civil war. Their first act was to remove the collector of the port, who was a Catholic, and therefore ineligible, and to appoint in his place four commissioners, all Protestants, to perform his duties. Scarcely had they begun, however, when Leisler, at the head of a body of militia, marched in and peremptorily ordered them out of the room. Bayard sternly reminded him that they were there by order of the king, and that resistance to them would be high treason, and punishable with death. Leisler in reply began a long speech in which the words "rogues," "traitors," and "devils" were freely applied to the commissioners. Even while he was speaking one of his soldiers seized a commissioner and dragged him into the street, where he was sadly beaten by the mob. Bayard himself was attacked, but succeeded in beating off his assailants and escaping to a house near by, which was at once besieged by the mob; he, however, contrived to elude them and regain his own house. Then the rabble paraded the streets, hooting and shouting for the blood of the aristocrats. Their slogan was, "The rogues have sixty men sworn to kill Captain Leisler." Bayard's friends came to him next morning, told him what passions were moving the commonalty, and besought him to flee from the city; he was at length persuaded, and succeeded in escaping to Albany. Van Cortlandt remained, and continued to act as mayor until the next October, when his house was attacked, and he was forced to flee for safety to Governor Treat of Connecticut.

Leisler was now sole master of the city, and with his lieutenant and ally, Millborne, committed many more acts of violence and oppression; but at last retribution came. As soon as King William's ministers turned their attention to New York's affairs, they wrote a letter to Lieutenant Governor Nicholson, ordering him to assume the government, call the leading citizens to his assistance, and "do and perform all the requirements of the office," they supposing him at the time to be in New York, whereas he was, as we have seen, on the sea. By some fatality this letter was not addressed to him by name, but simply to "Our Lieutenant Governor and Commander in Chief of our Province of New York in America, and in his absence to such as, for the time being, take care for preserving the peace and administering the laws in our said Province of New York in America." Leisler refused to allow the council to receive this letter. The king, he said, knew that he was at the head of the government, and intended the letter for him.

The council protested, but Leisler had the men at arms and the guns, and the messenger delivered the packet to him, whereupon he turned upon the councilors, called them popishly affected dogs and rogues, and bade them begone; he then proclaimed that the king had appointed him lieutenant governor, and at once entered on the duties of the office, named a council and other officers, had William and Mary proclaimed a second time, and on the Sabbath rode to the Dutch church and sat in the governor's pew, while his councilors seated themselves in the pew reserved for the magistrates.

Meantime Lieutenant Governor Nicholson had reached London and laid his case before the king and the committee on plantations, who sustained him in all that he had done; but as he had been embroiled in the factional fights there, they did not name him governor of New York, but made him lieutenant governor of Virginia. Colonel Henry Sloughter was appointed governor of New York, but owing to the Irish troubles and other causes did not reach his government until nearly a year had elapsed. Leisler, having secured the chief authority, was placated to a certain extent, so that Van Cortlandt, Colonel Bayard, and other exiles ventured to return to their families; but they were not long left in peace.

In the winter of 1690, having reason to suspect that these gentlemen had sent letters of complaint to the king, Leisler seized the Boston post rider as he rode through Westchester, confiscated his mail bag, and found among its contents, as he had expected, letters from Van Cortlandt, Bayard, and others complaining bitterly of his acts. He at once proclaimed that he had discovered a "hellish conspiracy" against his government, and that Colonel Bayard was the instigator of it. He therefore sent a file of soldiers, who seized that unfortunate gentleman, loaded him with chains, and thrust him into the common jail, where he received the same treatment as was meted out to the worst malefactors. Another file was sent against Van Cortlandt, who escaped, but William Nicolls, attorney-general of the province, was seized and thrust into the same prison with Colonel Bayard. They languished in jail many months.

By the summer of 1690 complaints, petitions, and addresses from the people of New York began to rain in upon King William, beseeching him to deliver them from the oppressor. These came not only from the English, but from the Dutch residents of New York. One was signed by the Dutch and French clergymen as well as by leading citizens. William, aroused by them, told Governor Sloughter that he must proceed to New York at once, and bring peace and order to the distracted city. Sloughter complied, and in December, 1690, sailed in the frigate *Archangel*, while Major Richard

Ingoldsby, the lieutenant governor, followed in the *Beaver;* two smaller vessels accompanied them. With Governor Sloughter sailed two companies of soldiers, and all the petitions, complaints, and documents in the case of Leisler were given him, with orders to make a careful and impartial investigation of the whole matter.

Sloughter also bore a system of government for the province, which differed little from that of James, and continued in force to the Revolution. It provided for a governor and council to be appointed by the king, and an assembly to be elected by the people. All peaceable persons "except papists" were assured liberty of conscience, but the Church of England was made the state church and placed under the jurisdiction of the Bishop of London. The members of the old King James council were nearly all retained and confirmed in their offices.

News of the sailing of the fleet came to New York by way of Boston, and its arrival was anxiously awaited by all parties. At last, on January 29, 1691, a sail was sighted far down the Narrows, then a second and third, and it was known that the long-expected fleet had arrived; but the fourth sail did not appear, and this laggard, most unfortunately for all parties, was the *Archangel*, the vessel that bore the governor and all the papers and commissions. Scarcely had the *Beaver* anchored and saluted the fort ere she was boarded by Phillipse and other members of the Nicholson government, who inquired eagerly for the governor.

"I know not where he is," said Ingoldsby; "we were separated these many days back by a great storm, and where the *Archangel* is, or whether she be at the bottom of the sea, no man may tell."

This was a great disappointment; yet they tried to induce the lieutenant governor to act. Rapidly they sketched the condition of affairs in the city,—the sufferings of the poor prisoners, the discontent of the people under Leisler's harsh government, the latter's high-handed acts of treason and violence,—and urged Ingoldsby to make a demand at once for the fort and government. The latter consented, and sent a messenger to Leisler demanding the fort for the king's soldiers and stores.

"Your authority?" replied Leisler.

"My ships and my soldiers," was the quick response.

But Leisler would not yield; he must see the lieutenant governor's commission from the king; but this was in the *Archangel* with Sloughter, as Leisler well knew. Uncertain how to act, Ingoldsby remained cooped up in his ships for several days, afraid to land, since Leisler had the fort and the troops; but at length, on being assured that the people were with him, he disembarked his soldiers and took post in the City Hall, which Leisler had offered for that purpose. When safely installed there he sent a letter to Leisler ordering him to release Bayard and Nicolls (still confined in the fort), because they had been named as members of his Majesty's council; but this threw Leisler into a terrible rage.

"What! those popish dogs and rogues?" he cried, and returned word that he should hold them until his Majesty's further orders arrived.

Six weeks now passed, this condition of things being

maintained, the king's lieutenant governor in the City Hall, his authority defied, and the king's councilors in the common jail.

At length Leisler committed an overt act of treason and murder. Learning that Ingoldsby and the councilors had gathered a force of several hundred men in the city, he sent them word to disperse under pain of being attacked and destroyed. Two hours to consider were given; but the governor replied at once. He should preserve the peace, he said, and whoever should attack him would render themselves public enemies to the crown of England.

At the time the message was sent Ingoldsby's two companies were drawn up on the "Parade," probably the Bowling Green, and Leisler, on receiving the reply, ordered a gun to be trained on them at once and fired; several shots were also sent into a house where the soldiers lodged. When the smoke cleared away it was seen that two British soldiers had been killed by the fire and several wounded. The English fired at the fort in return, but injured no one.

Happily, next day, as the parties stood confronting each other, the *Archangel* was signaled in the lower bay. Word was quickly sent to Governor Sloughter, who hurried to the city in a pinnace, and went to the City Hall, where his commission was immediately read, although it was dark when he arrived. Both the governor and council, except the two imprisoned in the fort, then took the oath of office.

It was eleven o'clock at night, but Ingoldsby was at once sent with his soldiers to the fort to demand its surrender in the name of the king. But Leisler would not comply until he had sent Sergeant Stoll, who had met the governor in England, to identify him as the real Sloughter. Stoll gravely told the governor that he was glad to find in him the same man he had known at home.

"Yes," said the governor, "I have been seen in England, and now intend to be seen in New York."

He refused to treat with Stoll, however, and again sent Ingoldsby to the fort to demand its surrender and to order Leisler and his council to report forthwith to the governor, and to bring Bayard and Nicolls with them. But Leisler refused, declaring it would be against all military precedent to deliver up a fort at midnight. A third time the messenger was sent, and a third time he was "contemptuously refused." Then governor and councilors retired with an agreement to meet at an early hour next morning.

They were very early at the City Hall. During the night the governor had matured his plans. Ignoring a humble letter from Leisler in which the latter asserted his loyalty and offered to "give an exact account of all his acts," he ordered Ingoldsby to go to the fort and command the men at arms to submit, promising pardon to all but Leisler and his council. When this was done the men laid down their arms and gave up Leisler and his councilors, who were led prisoners to the City Hall. Then the heavy doors of the cells in the fort were thrown back, and Bayard and Nicolls brought forth, aged and worn to skeletons almost by their thirteen months of captivity. They were met with good wishes, mingled with expressions of pity, and conducted to the City Hall, where they took the oath of office amid the cheers of the people. But Leisler and his councilors were thrust into the cells that had just been vacated by their victims; the chain that Bayard had worn was put on the leg of Leisler.

Soon the people began to clamor for the punishment of Leisler and his friends. A speedy trial was demanded by the accused and granted by Sloughter. On March 23, three days after the surrender, the prisoners were examined and bound over for trial. The case was at once given to the grand jury, which found a true bill against Leisler, Millborne, and eight others, charging them with " holding by force the king's fort against the king's governor, after publication of his commission, and after demand had been made in the king's name, and in the reducing of which lives had been lost."

The court sat March 30, and the trial proceeded for eight days with all the solemnity and stately ceremonial common in those days. A very august tribunal it was, too, of ten stern judges in flowing black robes and powdered, full-bottomed wigs—Dudley, the chief justice of the province, Thomas Johnson, Sir Robert Robinson, former governor of Bermuda, Jasper Hicks, captain of the *Archangel*, Lieutenant Governor Ingoldsby, Colonel William Smith, Major John Lawrence, Recorder Pinhorn, John Young, and Isaac Arnold—men chosen because they had suffered little or nothing from the prisoners, and who would be more likely, therefore, to judge them fairly.

When brought before them Leisler and Millborne

declined to plead at all until the court should decide whether the king's letter to Nicholson conferred the government upon Leisler. The court referred the question to Governor Sloughter and his council, and they declared in writing that neither in the king's letter nor in the papers of the privy council was there the slightest authority for the prisoner to seize upon the government. This swept away any defense the prisoners may have hoped to make; for unless they could prove authority they stood convicted of treason and murder, the penalty of which was death.

They did the very best thing possible under the circumstances—they refused to plead and appealed to the king. The eight other prisoners pleaded not guilty. Notwithstanding, the trial proceeded. Leisler, Millborne, and six of the other prisoners were found guilty; two were acquitted; and Chief Justice Dudley, assuming the black cap, passed sentence of death upon the eight.

But Sloughter hesitated to order their execution; he had grave doubts as to his authority to sign a death warrant in the case of an appeal to the king. "Never greater villains lived," he wrote King William, "but I am resolved to wait your pleasure, if by any other means than hanging I can keep the people quiet."

But he soon found that there was no other way. Scores of petitions and remonstrances from Dutch and English, and even from the Indians, against clemency were thrust upon him. So many had suffered grievous wrongs, either in person or property, from the usurper that the demand for his execution was general. The two Dutch clergymen are said to have openly advocated his death from the pulpit. Ladies of high station, sufferers from Leisler's tyranny, pleaded with the governor to sign the death warrant; the most eminent and loyal men of the province said to him that there could be no peace nor quietness while the leaders lived, and threatened to remove from the country unless the sentence was carried out. On the other hand, there came many petitions from the friends and families of the condemned, praying for clemency, so that between them the poor governor was nearly at his wit's end. But one day there came news from Albany that the Mohawk Indians, whom Leisler had greatly angered by his acts, had threatened to join the French as allies unless their enemy was executed.

On receipt of this news the governor and council met, and resolved that for the satisfaction of the Indians and to quiet the province it was necessary that the sentence against the principal offenders " be forthwith executed." This was laid before the House of Representatives, which the governor had convened, and that body indorsed the action of the governor and council. Sloughter therefore signed the death warrant, and Leisler and Millborne were executed.

The former met his fate with firmness and dignity. In his speech upon the gallows he begged that all discord and dissension about him might be buried with his ashes, and declared that in all he had done his sole aim had been to advance " the interests of William and Mary, and of the Reformed Protestant churches of these parts."

Perhaps the fairest judgment that could be passed

upon this puzzling character is that he was of unbalanced mind, half crazed by fear of aristocratic and popish plots and by the possession of unlimited power. Regarded from any standpoint, it was a most unfortunate affair, and retarded the growth of the colony not a little. For, despite Leisler's prayer, the spirit of faction survived his death, and for half a century the "Leislerites," as they were called, continued to exercise a disturbing influence on the politics of the city.

When the matter came before King William on Leisler's appeal he decided that the sentence was a righteous one and sustained the judges. On the ground of former loyal services rendered by Leisler, however, he restored to the latter's heirs his estates, which had been confiscated for treason, and four years later Parliament, on the petition of the friends of Leisler, "to promote peace and heal the scars of the civil war," reversed the decree of attainder which had been pronounced against Leisler, thus removing the attaint from his family.

## IX. THE APPROACH OF THE REVOLUTION.

FROM 1691 to 1764 the history of New York presents no events of great importance. During this period she grew in wealth, population, and commerce but slowly, the acts of the British government greatly restricting her foreign trade, and the many wars with the French and Indians on the north retarding her growth in numbers. Politically this period was marked by the almost constant struggle of her people for more liberty—liberty of trade, liberty to govern themselves, liberty of speech, and a free press. Some striking incidents and romantic phases of the period may be touched upon briefly.

Governor Sloughter died suddenly about two months after the execution of Leisler,—some said from poison,—and in 1692 was succeeded by Colonel Benjamin Fletcher. This gentleman was a brave soldier who had seen service in the Low Countries; he was a courtier too, shrewd, pliant, persuasive, politic, not to be praised for all that he did, but perhaps the best man for the place that could have been found. He allayed in a measure the angry passions that had been aroused in Leisler's time; he soothed and pacified the Indians, and he practically founded the Trinity Church of to-day, by giving it the revenues of the King's Farm, which belonged to him as governor; indeed, the inscription on the first Trinity Church built in New York, completed in 1696, stated that it was chiefly "enriched and promoted by the bounty of his Excellency Colonel Benjamin Fletcher."

During Governor Fletcher's reign the privateers brought a great deal of booty to New York. "King William's War," between France and England, which broke out in 1688-1689, put many of this class upon the seas. A privateer was a private vessel commissioned by its government to go out and capture on the high seas an enemy's vessel wherever it might be found. But many of them when once at sea captured all vessels, whether friend or foe, and thus became pirates, and the common enemies of mankind. It was the scandal of Governor Fletcher's reign that these pirates were permitted to harbor in the city equally with the privateers, and often in the guise of their more honest brethren. Both classes brought great store of wealth to the city—East India goods, rare fabrics of Teheran and Samarkand, Arabian gold, ivory, and slaves from the African coast. The pirate captains were marked figures on the streets. One of them is described as having been a slight, dark man of about forty, who scattered gold with prodigality.

He wore a uniform "rich and elegant, a blue cap with a band of cloth of silver, a blue jacket bordered with gold braid and garnished with large buttons of mother-of-pearl." He wore loose trousers of white linen, gathered at the knee into curiously clocked stockings. A long chain of Arabian gold was thrown about his neck, and in his knitted waistbelt gleamed a dagger, its hilt set with sparkling diamonds. Men accoutered like this, treating everybody who would drink to huge draughts of Sopus ale, and throwing golden louis d'ors about as carelessly as stivers, were familiar objects in New York at that time.

But the East India Company, which owned many of the vessels captured by them, soon made bitter complaint to the home government, alleging that the pirates were harbored in New York, and their ill-gotten booty purchased by her merchants; and as Colonel Fletcher was not very successful in catching them, he was recalled, and Richard, Earl of Bellomont, an Irish nobleman of the highest character, who had been very active against the freebooters, was appointed captain general of New York and New England, with special orders to stamp out piracy.

But Bellomont did not make a very successful governor. He was too austere, cold, bigoted, prejudiced; he arrived with the fixed idea that the chief men of the colony, including Fletcher, were imbued with piracy, and had no hesitation in so stating publicly. Almost his first official act was a very unwise one: he restored to the families of Leisler and Millborne their estates that had been forfeited, and as these had by this time passed into the hands of third parties, who had bought legally, the attempt to evict them nearly caused a riot, and at once excited factional feelings that had nearly died out. He did not show any greater tact in his attempts to suppress piracy and smuggling, and to recover from the great landed proprietors and the churches the large grants of land which Fletcher had given them. To stamp out the former he seized goods and arrested persons simply on suspicion, dismissed the highest officials without a hearing, and removed members of the council to fill their places with men of his own party. To remedy the latter evil he prepared a bill vacating all land grants made by former governors, and prohibiting any one person from holding over one thousand acres of land. One of the grants aimed at by this law was that of Domine Dellius, a Dutch Reformed clergyman of Albany, who had first secured it from the Indians, and later had had it confirmed by Fletcher; another was the grant to Trinity Church. Because of this zeal without knowledge the governor very soon had arrayed against him the clergy, the principal men of the colony, the merchants, and the king's officers. His only friends were the Leislerites, and soon the province was torn with the quarrels of the factions. Colonel Fletcher meantime was clamoring to have his accounts with the colony settled, that he might go to England with his vouchers and have his conduct as governor investigated by the Lords of Trade. Having served under the crown for thirty-five years without reproach, he said, he did not think he should become a castaway in the rear of his days.

Governor Bellomont died suddenly on the 5th of March, 1701, and was buried under the chapel of the fort. What would have been the outcome of his government had he lived it is impossible to say; as it was, he left the colony in much worse condition than he found it.

King William died on March 8, 1702, and was succeeded by Queen Anne of the Stuart line, who proved so excellent a ruler that her subjects called her "good Queen Anne." She was very charitable, especially to the struggling colonial churches. Among other gifts she bestowed on Trinity Church, in 1705, the Annetje Jans estate, a tract of some sixty acres lying above Chambers Street, on the west side of Broadway, which now, with the King's Farm before mentioned, yields princely revenues.

In 1725 quite an event occurred in the birth of the first newspaper New York had ever seen—the "Gazette."

New York in 1720.

It was but a mite when compared with our present mammoth editions, being printed on a half sheet of foolscap paper. It contained almost no local news, foreign letters and customhouse entries taking up most of the space. William Bradford, printer to the government, was editor and proprietor.

After nine years the "Gazette" found a rival in a new paper called the "Weekly Journal," and edited by John Peter Zenger. Zenger was a German Protestant who had been forced from his home on the Rhine by the armies of France, and coming to this country with Governor Hunter in 1710, a mere lad, had been apprenticed to William Bradford. Now grown to manhood, he turned his guns on his former teacher; for the "Journal," being the organ of the Whig or people's party, was bitterly opposed to the "Gazette," which was the organ of the governor and council, the conservatives, the vested interests. Whatever the "Journal" could do to bring into contempt the "aristocrats," as it called the governor and his party, it did. It attacked the governor, the council, the assemblymen—everybody and everything connected with the ruling class. Squibs, lampoons, ballads, witticism, satire, whatever would serve its purpose, all were made use of without stint. At last the people had an organ in which to make their wants and grievances known, and they appreciated it; it was the forerunner of the "Heralds," "Tribunes," "Suns," "Worlds," and "Journals" of a later period.

Bradford replied, defending the governor and his party; but his editorials lacked the pith and vigor of Zenger's, as you will see if you go to the public library and ask to see the journals in question. At length the government did what was best calculated to heighten the people's respect for their editor and increase his influence: it declared four issues of the "Weekly Jour-

nal " " libelous," and ordered them burned by the public
hangman, at the same time directing the mayor and
aldermen, who were of the popular party, to attend and
witness the ceremony. But the spirit of resistance was
abroad, and the mayor and magistrates refused to obey
the order; they said it was arbitrary and without warrant of law. Then Governor Cosby, a weak man, and
his advisers went still further: they seized Zenger and
threw him into prison on a charge of criminal libel.
Where he had had one friend before he now had ten.
Men rallied not so much to his aid as to the defense of
a free press, and to the right of the people to criticise
their officials. The excitement spread to the neighboring colonies, where the issue of the trial was awaited
with the greatest interest. The leaders of the popular
party in New York at this time were two lawyers named
James Alexander and William Smith; both at once volunteered to defend Zenger. Smith had been recorder
of the city, and was noted for his captivating eloquence;
Alexander had been surveyor general, and was also
noted for legal ability as well as for his silver tongue.
Unfortunately, their zeal led them to make a grave mistake at the outset: they boldly challenged the legality
of the commissions of Chief Justice de Lancey and of
Justice Phillipse, the two judges who composed the
court that was to try Zenger, on the ground that they
were not worded in the usual form, and had been issued
by Governor Cosby without consent of the council.

Judge de Lancey was of Huguenot ancestry, of the
aristocratic party, stout, florid, pompous in manner, a
great stickler for the dignity and prerogatives of his

office, and held this plea of the attorneys to be a gross contempt of court. As soon as he could command his voice, he said: "You have brought it to that pass, sirs, that either we must go from the bench or you from the bar," and he excluded them from further practice, assigning John Chambers to defend Zenger. There was no appeal for the disbarred attorneys in that day; but they were men of resources, and they hastened to Philadelphia, and secured, to assist Chambers, Andrew Hamilton, reputed the ablest and most eloquent advocate then in the colonies. At the same time, through the press and by private conversation in the clubs and coffeehouses, they made public the story of their own wrongs and the merits and demerits of the case.

When the trial was called, in July, 1735, Hamilton appeared eager for the fray, and was greeted with shouts of approval by the people, who saw in him the champion of popular rights. His first reply to the indictment was that the articles in the "Journal" could not be libelous, because they were *true*. Bradley, the king's attorney general, took exception to this plea, and quoted the old English law that even the truth if repeated with intent to injure another was libelous, and punishable as such.

So all summer the legal battle raged with varying fortunes to the combatants, and all summer the entire body of the colonies watched and waited to see if the press was to be muzzled, or left to be the Argus-eyed exposer of official corruption, and the defender of the people's rights. At length, after a charge by the judge unfavorable to the prisoner, the case was given to the jury, who, after being out but a few moments, returned with a verdict of " Not guilty."

The people received it with shouts of approval, and were so delighted that they would have borne Hamilton to his hotel on their shoulders, but he would not permit it. The corporation, however, tendered him a banquet, at which he was presented by the mayor with the freedom of the city in a gold box; and the same evening a grand ball was given in his honor. In this first openly avowed and distinct contest for their rights, the people won a great victory.

The closing days of British rule in New York were marked by the founding of one of the city's noblest institutions, Columbia College. By 1751, after many years of effort, the sum of £3,443 had been raised by lottery and public subscription to found a college in New York, and a bill was passed by the legislature naming ten trustees to take charge of it.

King's College in 1758.

In 1752 the vestry of Trinity Church offered to give a site and the necessary grounds for a campus. This offer was accepted, and in 1753 the trustees invited the Rev. Dr. Samuel Johnson, an eminent clergyman of that day, to be the first president. His salary was £250 a year. The college was first opened in the autumn of 1753, in the vestry room of Trinity Church, with an entering class of ten. On August 23, 1756, the corner stone of a new building was laid by Governor Charles Hardy with appropriate ceremonies. Its site and grounds covered the whole block now bounded by College Place, Barclay, Church, and Murray streets, and the new building was first opened to students in May, 1760. During the Revolution no sessions were held, the building being used by the British as a hospital. On the return of peace the college was reorganized and its name changed from King's to Columbia.

## X. THE PEOPLE UNDER BRITISH RULE.

VERY soon after the British came the tone of society in New York was almost wholly changed, the English language, customs, and manners largely supplanting the Dutch. New York, with the large influx of immigrants from England and the New England States, became a miniature London, English to the core. She celebrated with fête and procession the birthdays of the king, queen, and members of the royal family. She donned the outward and visible signs of mourning at their decease. The governor and his official family, the officers of the garrison, the patroons, professional men, and retired merchants formed an upper or court circle and gave tone to society. In place of the simple, domestic, democratic social system of the Dutch came in the English one of classes. London fashions soon became popular, although, as William Smith, a local historian, observed, " by the time we adopt them they become disused in England." London tradesmen, tailors, peruke makers, and teachers came with them, and greater elegance in dress, equipage, houses, and furniture was the result.

Among the distinguished company that accompanied Governor Andros in 1678 was the Rev. James Wooley, who had recently taken holy orders, and who had been commissioned chaplain to the king's army in New York. This gentleman used his eyes and ears to good purpose, and on his return to London wrote a little book called "A Two Years' Journal in New York," which gives some pleasant glimpses of the social life of our city at that time (1678-1680). "The country," he wrote, "is of a sweet and wholesome breath, free from those annoyances which are commonly ascribed by naturalists to the insalubrity of any country, viz., south or southeast winds, stagnant waters, lowness of shoals, inconstancy of weather, and the excessive heat of the summer; it is gently refreshed, fanned, and allayed by constant breezes from the sea."

The people he found very friendly and hospitable, though "a clan of high-flown religionists." The two domines, the Lutheran and Dutch Reformed, he found it necessary to rebuke for their unfriendly and unchristian attitude toward each other. He passes to this description of what was then a favorite recreation:

"We had a very good diversion in an orchard of Mr. John Robinson of New York, where we *followed a bear from tree to tree*, upon which he could swarm like a cat; and when he was got to his resting place, perched upon a high branch, we dispatched a youth after him with a club to an opposite bough, who knocking his paws, he comes grumbling down backward with a thump, so we after him again."

Every New Year's day, Mr. Wooley tells us, the English observed "a neighborly commerce of presents." One sent him a sugar loaf, another a pair of gloves, a third a bottle or two of wine.

One day he saw "two Dutch boors" grappling under his window. "I called up an acquaintance and asked him to fetch a kit full of water and discharge it at them, which immersion cooled their courage and loosed their grip. So we used to part our mastiffs in England."

The city of New York he described as being "as large as some market towns with us, and all built the London way." "The diversion, especially in the winter season and by the Dutch, is aurigation, i.e., riding about in wagons [probably straw rides]; . . . and upon the ice it is admirable to see men and women as it were flying upon their skates from place to place with markets [baskets] upon their heads and backs."

When our author returned he took with him as souvenirs "a gray squirrel, a parrot, and a raccoon."

While Mr. Wooley was preaching to the garrison in the fort there arrived in New York two young men in queer scallop hats and long coats, who had been sent from Germany by a sternly religious Protestant order there—the Labadists—to find a location in this country for one of their communities. These men were clever, with a great thirst for knowledge, and went prying all over the country, letting nothing escape their eyes and pens and pencils.

In New York they were "regaled on milk and peaches, fish and fruit." The most interesting part of their book to us describes a tour they made through the length and breadth of the present borough of Brooklyn in October, 1679. Crossing the ferry on September 29, they climbed a hill, and then rode "along open roads and woody places, and through a village called Breuckelen, which has a small ugly church standing in the middle of the road."

That night they spent in the farmhouse of one Simon de Hart, and had for supper a roasted haunch of venison, a goose, a wild turkey, and oysters both raw and roasted, and they sat up with their host late into the night before a great hickory fire that roared hospitably up the chimney. From his house they visited New Utrecht, and were received by Jacques Cortelyou, who lived in a stone house, one of several in the village, and united the callings of land surveyor, mathematician, and doctor of medicine. Because of illness in their host's family they were obliged to sleep in the barn, which they did on straw spread with sheepskins, "amid the continual grunting of hogs, squealing of pigs, bleating and coughing of sheep, barking of dogs, crowing of cocks, and cackling of hens." After several days they leisurely retraced their steps to New York, noting on the way the Indian villages, the wild grapes, peach orchards, and fields of watermelons. This Cortelyou house will again appear in our story.

The era of the privateers and "Red Sea men," who flooded the city with East India goods and Arabian gold (1700–1705), was marked by the most lavish display and extravagance. Broadway of a Sunday morning must then have presented a brilliant and animated spectacle as the throng of fair women and courtly men moved along it on the way to service. Trinity, or "the English church," first opened in 1696, and the new Dutch church on Garden Street, built in 1693, were then the fashionable places of worship, though Trinity, as the church of the court circle, took precedence.

Among the distinguished company are Governor Lord Bellomont, tall and stern, James de Lancey, the lawyer, who will be later chief justice and lieutenant gov-

"Broadway of a Sunday morning."

ernor, Isaac de Riemer, the Huguenot and mayor of the city, Colonel Nicholas Bayard and Mrs. Bayard, Dr. Samuel Staats and his wife, a beautiful East Indian princess, Frederick Phillipse, Gabriel Minvielle, Thomas Willett, Richard Townley, and John Lawrence, of the king's council, James Graham and James Emott, the distinguished lawyers, Abraham Gouverneur, George

Heathcote, Johannes and Abraham de Peyster, and other able men of that day.

And how were they dressed? Certain old family inventories enable us to describe their costumes with as much detail as though we were a society reporter of 1705 sent out for the purpose. Colonel Bayard, for instance, wears a long-skirted, cinnamon-colored cloth coat, embroidered four or five inches deep with silver lace, and lined with sky-blue silk; his waistcoat is of red satin inwoven with gold; his breeches are of the same color and material as his coat, and are trimmed with silver braid at the pockets and knees. His lower limbs and feet are covered with dove-colored stockings of silk and low shoes set off with bright silver buckles. His broad-brimmed black hat of felt is adorned with a band of gold lace. His full-bottomed wig is sprinkled with starch finely ground and sifted, to which burnt alabaster or whiting has been added to give it body, and is scented with ambergris. The ends of his "steenkirk," or neckcloth of fine muslin, are laced and tucked into his expansive shirt bosom; the latter being of fine holland adorned with colbertine ruffles, to display which the waistcoat is left open. His snuff is daintily scented, and contained in an elegant ivory box with an invisible hinge and a looking-glass in the lid.

When he has occasion to use his handkerchief we see that it is of the finest silk and ornamented with the British arms, while on its folds are printed or painted the ensigns and standards captured from the French, perhaps in some action at which the colonel was present. And when he draws forth his watch to note the hour we notice the beautiful shagreen case studded with gold which protects it, and which has his seal and watch key attached by a wide silk ribbon. He flourishes a cane with an elegant gold head engraved with crown and cipher; but his diamond-hilted sword with its gay sword knot, which every gentleman wears when fully dressed, has been left behind because of the sacred character of the day.

The other gentlemen are dressed in the same style, although there is a pleasing variety in color and material.

If the gentlemen are thus brilliant, the ladies appear brilliant as emperor moths. Mrs. Bayard, for instance, wears in place of a bonnet a "frontage," a kind of head-dress made of rows of plaited muslin reënforced with wire, one rising above the other, and growing smaller as they rise. She also wears the steenkirk. The bodice of her purple-and-gold atlas gown is laced over very tight stays, and the gown itself is cut away in front to display the black velvet petticoat, edged with two silver orrices, and high enough to show the green silk stockings and richly embroidered shoes of fine morocco with red clocks. Her hair is also powdered, and she is perfumed with rose water and *eau de Carne*. Some of the younger ladies are even more richly dressed. Dr. Staats's stately East Indian princess appears in purple and gold; a pretty little lady behind her wears a satin gown over an Alijah petticoat striped with green, gold, and white; another gown is flowered with green and gold, over a scarlet-and-gold atlas petticoat edged with silver.

As the last tones of the bell cease the brilliant company is lost in the churches, and the street is left to Indians and negro slaves.

The latter were an important element of the population all through colony days and for some years after the Revolution. We meet them everywhere—in the fields, on the streets, bringing water, marketing, serving, herding, doing most of the menial work of the town. There were three classes of slaves—negroes, Indians, and white immigrants, or redemptioners. The negroes were mostly native Africans imported direct from Angola or Madagascar, or indirectly from the West Indies in the colony vessels. They still preserved their native savagery, and were an element of fear to the more timorous. Twice there was an uprising among them, in 1712 and 1741, and a plot, as was charged, to murder all the males and capture the town; but both were easily put down. The Indian slaves were probably captives taken in war or condemned to servitude for petty crimes. The Europeans were those who agreed with the captains who gave them a passage over to serve a certain time after landing until the passage money should be discharged by their wages. To prove these statements take the following advertisements from newspapers of the day:

In 1751: "Likely negroes, men and women, imported from the coast of Africa, . . . to be sold by Thomas Grenell."

In 1732: "Just arrived from Great Britain and to be sold on board the ship *Alice and Elizabeth*, Captain Paine commander, several likely Welsh and English serving men, most of them tradesmen."

In 1747: "Run away on April the 25th, from Captain

Abraham Kip in New York, an Indian man about eighteen years old and speaks good English."

Having seen the Dutch city, we shall wish to visit it now under its English masters, and note the changes that have occurred. It has certainly grown and solidified, so to speak, since our visit in 1664, a hundred

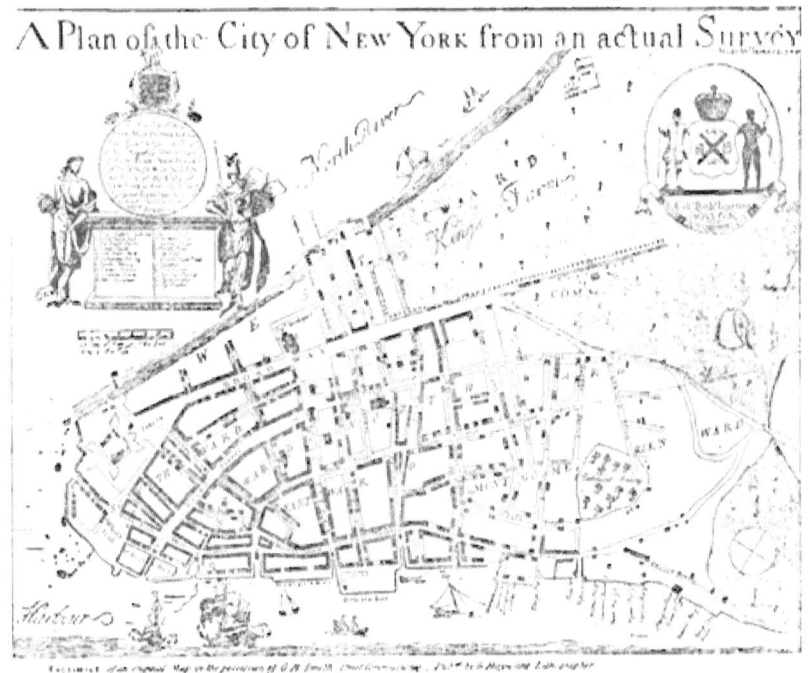

years ago. The city now has crept north as far as Warren Street on the west, and Chatham on the east, while a village plot appears on the west of the "High Road to Boston" (the present Bowery). There is a new wall of palisades extending from the East River through Franklin Square and "the Swamp" to the line of the present Canal Street, and thence to the North River, with a blockhouse and gates at Chatham Street, Broadway, and the waterside. The great pond called the Kolch, or Collect (on the site of the present Tombs and to the eastward of it), still remains, while the Swamp (now devoted to the busy warehouses of the hide and leather men)[1] is covered with tan vats and tanneries.

The Battery in 1746.

Most of the streets within the city limits are paved, and lighted by lanterns suspended from every seventh house. There is a fire company of "four and twenty able-bodied men," and two fire engines " of Mr. Newnham's patent," the latter just imported from London,

---

[1] This somewhat famous locality lay south of the present approach to the East River Bridge and west of Franklin Square, extending nearly to North William Street.

and a "rattle watch" that patrols the streets at night.

We will begin our stroll at the Battery. The fort is still there, very little changed, but it has a new name—Fort George—after the reigning king, for it is named anew with each new ruler that comes to the throne. It is still the seat of government. Here is the governor's dwelling, called the "Government House," and a garrison of regular troops—two lieutenants, one ensign, three sergeants, two drummers, a master gunner, one hundred privates, four "matrosses," a "chirurgeon" (surgeon), a storekeeper, and a chaplain. And the governor needs them all, for what with French and Indian descents from the north, rumors of popish plots, uprisings of slaves, and quarrels with the colonial legislature, his post is no sinecure.

His residence is also the social capitol, and "high doings" often took place there in the old colony days. No fête day, whether the anniversary of the birth of king, queen, or prince of the royal blood, the coming of an heir to the throne, the advent of a new governor, or a great national event, can pass without the holding of a grand ball at Government House, to which come the beauty and chivalry of the town. For instance, on October 30, 1734, it being the anniversary of his Majesty's birthday: "In the evening the whole city was illuminated. His Excellency and Lady gave a splendid ball and supper at the Fort, where was the most numerous and fine appearance of Ladies and Gentlemen that had ever been known upon the like occasion."

Imposing ceremonies had preceded this event:

"Between the hours of eleven and twelve in the forenoon, His Excellency our Governor was attended at his House in Fort George by the Council, Assembly, Merchants, and other Principal Gentlemen and Inhabitants of this and adjacent places. The Independent Companies posted here being under Arms, and the Cannon round the Ramparts firing while His Majesty's, the Queen's, the Prince's, and the Royal Families', and their Royal Highnesses the Prince and Princess of Orange's Healths were drunk, and then followed the Healths of His Grace the Duke of Newcastle, of the Duke of Grafton, of the Right Honorable Sir Robert Walpole, and many other Royal Healths."

At the coronation of King George, June 11, 1734, much the same ceremony was observed at the governor's mansion, and "afterwards His Excellency, attended by the Gentlemen of the Council, etc., went into the Field [the present City Hall Park], and received the Militia of the City drawn up there, and expressed great satisfaction at their order, discipline, and appearance, and was pleased to order twelve barrels of beer to be distributed among them to drink their Majesties' and the Royal Healths."

When a new governor came—which was pretty often—he was received with much state and ceremony. Thus when William Cosby arrived in July, 1732, he landed "about ten o'clock in the evening, and was received at the Waterside by several Gentlemen, who attended him to the Fort. The next day, between the Hours of eleven and twelve, His Excellency walked to the City Hall (a company of Halberdiers and a Troop of

Horse marching before, and the Gentlemen of His Majesty's Council, the Corporation, and a great number of Gentlemen and Merchants of this city following, the streets being lined on each side with the Militia), where his Commission was published [i.e., read], and then His Excellency returned, attended as before, back to the Fort. The Militia then drew up on the Parade and saluted him with three volleys."

Leaving the Battery and its memories, let us walk up

City Hall. Wall Street.

Broad Street to the corner of Nassau and Wall. The canal in the middle of Broad Street has been filled in, and the street itself is lined with handsome dwellings. At the northeast corner of the last-named streets (where now stands the gray granite pile of the Subtreasury, with its statue of Washington looking calmly on the hurrying crowds) is the new City Hall, which we shall refer to later as the cradle of national existence.

The city built it in 1700, at a cost of three thousand pounds, and sold the old City Hall, built by Kieft, for nine hundred and twenty pounds to help defray the cost. Here the Provincial Assembly and the governor's council hold their sessions, and the Supreme Court and the mayor's and admiralty courts meet. Here, too, the royal governors publish their commissions, and the new mayors also.

The latter ceremonies are attended with more pomp than in later days. Thus, Mayor Thomas Noell, who took the oath here in 1701, records in his diary:

"On Tuesday, the 14th day of October, 1701, I was commissioned and sworn Mayor of the City of New York, before the Honorable John Nanfan, Esq., Lieutenant Governor of this Province, and Council, in His Majesty's Fort, William Henry, and from thence according to the usual solemnity I went to Trinity Church, where was a sermon preached by Mr. Vesey, which ended, I went to the City Hall, attended by the Recorder, Aldermen, and Assistants, and other officers, when, after the ringing of three bells, I published my Commission, and then went up into the Courthouse, and took the chair, when Isaac de Riemer, Esq., the late Mayor, delivered to me the charter and seals of this city."

Visitors of distinction were usually received at the City Hall. Thus when Lord Augustus Fitz Roy arrived in 1732 to marry Governor Cosby's daughter, the mayor, aldermen, and assistants waited on him, attended by the chief officers of the city regiment, "and being introduced to his Lordship in the Council Chamber, the Recorder addressed himself to him in the name of the Corporation, congratulating his Lordship on his safe arrival, and returning the thanks of the city for the Honor they received by his Lordship's presence, as also for his Lordship's condescension in being pleased to become a member thereof. Then the Worshipful the Mayor presented his Lordship with the copy of his Freedom, to which was annexed the city seal inclosed in a curious Gold Box, with the arms of the city thereon neatly engraved; which his Lordship was pleased to receive with the greatest Goodness and Complaisance, and likewise to assure the Corporation that he should always entertain the kindest sentiments of this Expression of their Regard and Esteem for him."

This "gold box" was made by Charles Le Roux, the Tiffany of those days. His bill for it was for the gold (one ounce twelve pennyweights) £10 8s., and for "fashione and engraving the Box" £4, in all £14 8s., or over seventy dollars of our money. When Major Alexander Cosby, the governor's brother, and Thomas Freeman of London, visited the city the next year (1733-1734), that the latter might marry the governor's second daughter, the freedom of the city was tendered them in a silver "Guilt Box" that cost, for the two, £7 1s. 11½d.

At the head of Wall Street stands Trinity Church, erected in 1696, as before said, and greatly enlarged and improved in 1737. The first edifice is said to have been one hundred and forty-eight feet long by seventy-two feet wide, with a steeple, the pride of the city, one hundred and seventy-five feet high. Over the great door was a sonorous Latin inscription, which done into the English of that day read as follows:

"This Trinity Church was founded in the eighth year of the Most Illustrious Sovereign Lord William III., by the Grace of God, King of England, Scotland, France, and Ireland, Defender of the Faith, and in the year of our Lord 1696, and was built by the voluntary contributions and gifts of some persons, and chiefly enriched and promoted by the bounty of his Excellency Colonel Benjamin Fletcher, captain general and governor in chief of this province, in the time of whose government the inhabitants of this city, of the Protestant religion of the Church of England, as now established by law, were incorporated by a charter under the seal of the province; and many other valuable gifts he gave to it of his private fortune."

This edifice was destroyed in the great fire of 1776, and rebuilt in 1790. The present beautiful Gothic structure was built in 1846.

It is but a few steps down Wall Street to the water front, then, as later, one of the most fascinating portions of the city. To make its round in our own time is to come in contact with the tongues, costumes, and products of the wide earth. To a lesser extent this was the case in colonial times.

There are more docks, ships, and warehouses than we noticed in 1664. The pirates and privateersmen are the most picturesque, and in this long-roofed, low-porched tavern of Captain Benjamin Kierstede we shall probably find a score or more of them clustered about its box stove and spinning yarns after the manner of sailormen. We are struck by their resemblance to Whittier's sea dog:

> "Salt as the sea wind, tough and dried
> As a lean cusk from Labrador."

They are famous fighters, and prove an efficient arm of the service in these bitter French and Indian wars. The "London Magazine" of September, 1757, stated that since "the beginning of the war" (French and Indian War, 1755-1763) thirty-nine vessels, with one hundred and twenty-eight guns and one thousand and fifty men, had been fitted out to prey on French commerce; while a letter from a merchant in New York to a friend in London, of January 5, 1757, declares: "There are now thirty Privateers out of this Place, and ten more on the stocks and launched." The letter writer adds that up to that time (1757) these vessels had brought in fourteen prizes, valued at over one hundred thousand pounds.

The privateersmen were a brave, reckless, daredevil class. They displayed much ingenuity in inventing striking, terrible, or outré names for their vessels. Thus we read of the *Norfolk Revenge*, *Game Cock*, *Try-All*, *Favorite Betsey*, *Hook-Him-Snivey*, *Who'd-Have-Thought-It*, *Spitfire*, *Surprise*, *Eagle*, *Tyger*, *Royal Hunter*, *Tory's Revenge*, *Little Bob*, *Flying Harlequin*, *Revolution*, *Wheel-of-Fortune*, *Charming Polly*, *Charming Peggy*, *Dreadnaught*, *Hornet*, *Decoy*, and others. Many of them made fortunes in a few months and spent them as quickly. Thus the privateer brig *Clinton* captured the French ship *La Pomme*, with a cargo of indigo, cotton, and sugar valued at forty thousand pounds. The *Clinton* was out but six weeks, and every man before the mast received one hundred and sixty pounds' prize money. Furthermore, their captain, Bevan, had an " ox roasted whole and mixed a hogshead of punch for them in the fields."

No wonder that with such lures Governor Hamilton of New Jersey should complain that the privateer captains were sweeping into their ranks the flower of the youth of his province.

Many of the privateersmen turned pirates,—that is, attacked and took the ships of all nations,—and thus became the common enemies of mankind. The most famous of these was Captain William Kidd, who was a notable figure in New York in those days. When we first hear of him he was a reputable shipmaster, captain of the bark *Antigua*, trading between New York and London, and well known to the merchants of both as a bold and skillful navigator. In his certificate of marriage to " Sarah Oort, widow," in 1691, he is styled " Captain William Kidd, gentleman."

By 1694 the pirates had so increased in the Indian Ocean that they promised to sweep the ships of the East India Company from those seas, and that powerful company appealed to the English government for protection. But all the king's ships were engaged in the war with France then raging, and could not be spared to police those distant waters. This fact caused the king and admiralty to listen with favor to a plan now proposed to them by Captain Kidd through his friend and patron,

the great Robert Livingston of New York, which was to
fit out a private armed vessel, put it in charge of the
aforesaid Captain Kidd, and authorize him to beat up a
crew and go in search of the pirates. After some
persuasion the king consented. The *Adventure Galley*, a
large ship, was fitted out, and with seventy men, just
enough to man her, Kidd sailed for New York, arriving
in the spring of 1696. Here he had no difficulty in
securing one hundred more men from the class described,
and with them put to sea. But the wise old sea dogs
of the port shook their heads over the venture. They
said that when Captain Kidd got to sea, if he did not
find pirates to capture and provide prize money for his
crew, the latter would mutiny and become pirates themselves—which was what happened, if the story of Kidd
himself is to be believed. After patrolling the American coast for a while without result, Kidd bore up for
the Red Sea, and was not seen in New York for nearly
three years, although rumors that he had himself turned
pirate were freely bandied about. But in 1699 Kidd
sailed into Gardiners Bay, at the east end of Long
Island, and dispatched a message to Governor Bellomont
at New York. In it he said that his men had mutinied
and forced him to turn pirate; that he had left his " large
Moorish ship," the *Quidah Merchant*, in the West Indies,
and would deliver her up and a large amount of treasure
if he could be assured a free pardon. Bellomont, who
was in Boston when the message reached him, replied
that if Kidd could establish his innocence he should not
be molested. Kidd accordingly came to Boston, where
he was arrested, and after examination was sent to Eng-

land for trial. The trial was one of the most notable in the United Kingdom; it ended in his conviction, and his being hanged in chains in Execution Dock in 1701.

Such is the true story of Captain Kidd. Perhaps he never would have become famous but for the English balladmakers and our own masters of fiction, Irving and Poe.

But it is time that we continued our stroll. We will go north along Pearl Street, which, with the cross streets leading out of Broadway, is the shopping center—the Broadway, Sixth Avenue, Fourteenth Street, and Twenty-third Street of 1760. The stores are plain and unpretending. In many cases the shopkeeper's family lives above the store. They offer all sorts of wares for sale under one roof, like the modern department store. The Wanamaker's of New York at this time is the store of Adolph Phillipse, Esq., a great man indeed, with a house in town, a manor at Phillipseborough, who has been king's councilor, master in chancery, judge, and speaker of the Assembly. He is a great merchant, too, sending ventures as far as India, and having a large wholesale store as well as retail department. His store is a brick building three stories high, the lower story being devoted to the wholesale trade, and the second to the retail. The former is filled with country merchants as we enter, sampling and tasting. A prominent feature is the great oaken, iron-bound chest, in which, there being neither safe nor bank vault, are kept the money, wampum, pearls, and jewelry of the establishment.

The story above is well filled with the fair ladies of Manhattan, to whom the handsome merchant's rich

East India fabrics and English goods are a great attraction. They are pricing taffeta, paduasoy, silk, tabby, widow's crape, brocaded lutestring, flowered Spanish silk, India dimity, cherry derry, and the like, that modern merchants would no doubt find it difficult to produce.

But we will continue our walk north along Pearl Street, flourishing our "keanes," as the manner of men about town is. What a number of markets there are, long, low, open buildings roofed with tiles; the meal, fish, oyster, and meat markets, one at the foot of nearly every street. The Bear Market (now Washington), over on the North River front, was so called, it is said, because the first meat sold there was that of a bear shot while swimming the North River.

There are many quaint craftsmen on the "slips" and short streets crossing Pearl; for instance, this shop of Anthony Lamb in Old Slip, "at the sign of the Quadrant and Surveying Compass," where one can buy "quadrants, forestaffs, nocturnals, rectifiers, universal scales, gunters, sliding gunters, wood or brass box compasses," and so on for half a hundred instruments. At the house of William Bradford, "next door but one to the Treasurer's," lodges "Moses Slaughter, staymaker," from London, who offers "a parcel of extraordinary good and fashionable stays of his own making. Slaughter is anxious to suit those that want with extraordinary good stays." Another is the shop of John Wallace, "at the sign of the Cross Swords, next door to Mrs. Byfield, near the Fly Market," who "makes, mends, and grinds all sorts of knives, razors, scissors, and penknives, and surgeons' instruments," as well as "jacks, locks, keys, and stillards."

At the northwest corner of the Great Dock, " next door to the sign of the Leopard," Simon Franks of London has a small shop, " where he makes and sells all sorts of perukes after the best and newest fashion, and cuts and dresses ladies' wigs and towers."

The strangest shop, however, is that of Joseph Liddell, " Pewterer," " at the sign of the Platter, at the lower end of Wall Street near the Meal Market," who sells " pewter ware of all sorts, cannons, six and four pounders, and swivel guns, cannon shot, cart and wagon boxes," etc. " He will pay you hard money for old brass and pewter."

The undertaker has a most gruesome establishment. Coffins, some very ornate in silver and rosewood, stand on end in his warerooms. Over a bier at the farther end are spread the two parish palls, one of black velvet for general use, the other of cloth with a border of white silk a foot wide, designed only for unmarried men and maidens. On shelves around the sides of the room are flannel shrouds, gloves, scarfs, hatbands, and other articles of mourning costume. In a tray of lacquer work on the counter are the shopman's cards, which inform the public that he " hath a velvet pall, a good hears, mourning cloaks, and black hangings for rooms to be let at reasonable rates. He hath also for sale all sorts of mourning and half mourning, white silk for scarfs and hatbands at funerals, with coffins, shrouds, and all sorts of burying cloaths for the dead."

The signs are another striking feature of the streets.

They swing above every door, not bearing the name of the shopkeeper as with us, but the figure of some animal or object. The reason is that many of the people cannot read, but they can tell a shop by the sign of a Cart and Horse, a Bear, or a pair of Crossed Swords.

Thus the Unicorn and Mortar is a grocer's sign, a Chair Wheel of a chairmaker, a Dial of a clockmaker, the King's Arms of the Exchange Coffee House, the Scotch Arms of another tavern, while over Thomas Lepper's "Ordinary," opposite the Merchants' Coffee House, swings the sign of the Duke of Cumberland. He advertises a *table d'hôte* dinner at "half an hour after one." The Boston post puts up at the sign of the Black Horse in Upper Queen (now Pearl) Street. A Bunch of Grapes, Blue Ball, Dolphin, Two Cupids, Jamaica Pilot Boat, Rose and Crown, Fighting Cock, Spread Eagle, White Swan, the Sun, the Leopard, the Bible, are familiar and distinctive signs.

The coffeehouses, introduced from London, are quite numerous, and the favorite resorts of all classes. As a resident of the city at this time writes, "You have all manner of news there. You have a good fire which you may sit by as long as you please; you have a dish of coffee; you meet your friends for the transaction of business, and all for a penny, if you don't care to spend more."

The Exchange Coffee House is the most exclusive and elegant, the Merchants' the most popular and comfortable. Shall we enter? The floor is bare and sanded, the tables and chairs very plain, the prints on the walls very high-colored; but there is a pleasant fire, a perpetual supply of hot water, and the coffee and tea pots close by to keep warm. Here the Boston, Philadelphia, and New York newspapers (small two-page affairs filled mostly with extracts from London journals) are "taken

A Coffeehouse.

in." A gentleman is reading from one to a group of interested listeners as we enter:

"Last Thursday morning a creature of an uncommon size and shape was observed to break through a window of a storehouse of this city and jump into the street, where was suddenly a number of spectators, who followed it till it jumped over several high fences, and at last stuck between two houses, where they shot it. Many had a curiosity to view it, and say it was seven feet long. Most of them say it is a panther, but whence it came, or how it got into the storehouse, we are at a loss to know."

Odd, isn't it, the idea of chasing panthers around on lower Broadway and wedging them between buildings on Broad Street? It emphasizes the crowning glory of the American metropolis that all her wealth, beauty, solidity, civilization, has been wrested from forest and field in a little over two centuries and a half.

As we come up to Peck Slip there is an alarm of fire, and we step one side to see the Newnham fire engines with the volunteer firemen go by. The former have been recently in-

vented, and are force pumps worked by long handles, yet capable, we are told, of throwing a stream seventy feet high. Each requires twelve men to work it. A few years before (1736), the city had built a house for these engines near the "watchhouse" in Broad Street. The volunteer firemen were appointed by act of Assembly of September 19, 1738, their only salary being that they were not obliged to serve on juries, nor as constables, surveyors of highways, or militia.

In 1798 the city firemen were chartered as the Volunteer Fire Department, and so continued until 1865, when the present efficient system of a paid force took its place.

Here at Peck Slip we may take the ferryboat for Brooklyn. There is another running from the Fly Market at the foot of Maiden Lane, but both land at the modern Fulton Street, on the Brooklyn shore.

A picture of the day shows the dock and ferry house and the queer cattle boats with their one mast and spritsail forward. The passenger boats are also furnished with a sail, but when the wind is contrary it requires as long to make the ferry as in 1664, while the sudden gusts sweeping down the river sometimes capsize the boat. Timid passengers often wait two or three days for a favorable wind before venturing over.

The men of colonial times have perhaps impressed you as being stern, cold, formal, unsocial beings, rarely unbending from the restraint and dignity of official or business life; but in this you do them an injustice. They had their pleasures, the principal ones being theater going, card playing, dancing, horse racing, horseback riding, sailing, skating, athletic games and sports. There was a playhouse in New York as early as October, 1733, as we know by an advertisement of it in the New York "Gazette" of that date. A playbill in the "Weekly Post Boy" of March 12, 1750, informs the public that, "by His Excellency's permission," "the Historical Tragedy of Richard III. will be presented at the theater in Nassau Street, together with a farce called the Bean in the Sudds. Tickets to be had of the printer, pit 5s., gallery 3s. To begin precisely at half an hour after 6 o'clock, and no person to be admitted behind the scenes."

There were other entertainments, however. Thus in 1749 John Bonnin advertises his "Philosophical Optical Machine," which was to be exhibited at "eight o'clock in the morning and continue showing till nine at night." Then there was Punch's company of comedians, and a "New Pantomime Entertainment of Grotesque Characters in Mr. Holt's Long Room," and a "Concert of Vocal and Instrumental Musick at the House of Robert Tod, to begin precisely at five o'clock. Tickets at 5s." The most remarkable, however, was a new electrical machine, announced in the "Post Boy" of May 16, 1748, which showed "the most surprising effects or Phenomena on Electricity of attracting, repelling, and Flenemies Force, particularly the new way of electryfying several persons at the same time, so that Fire shall dart from all Parts of their Bodies."

But these merrymakings, balls, fêtes, and stately ceremonials passed with the court circle that made them possible, and a sterner age succeeded. In 1764 "the times that tried men's souls" were near at hand. Let us turn now to consider them and the honorable rôle that New York played in that heroic age.

## XI. THROWING OFF THE BRITISH YOKE.

IN March, 1765, the British Parliament passed the Stamp Act, the little entering wedge that first opened the breach between the American colonies and the mother country, England, a breach that was suffered to grow and widen through the folly and weakness of her king, George III., and the stupidity and wickedness of his ministers, until at last England lost her colonies, and they came into a free national existence.

In itself this Stamp Act was not so oppressive a measure. It simply enacted that all receipts, deeds, contracts, and other legal papers, even to marriage licenses, should be written or printed on stamped paper, which paper should be sold only by the collectors of revenue, and should form part of the tax to be collected from the colonies. Such a tax is a favorite mode of raising revenue to-day with several European governments, as well as with our own.

The difficulty with the colonists was that a principle, a right, was involved. In order to put ourselves in their place we must stop and consider how the Briton of that day prized and jealously guarded the British constitution. And well he might, for the people had secured that noble instrument by a thousand years of struggle with kings and nobles. First came Magna Charta, the

Great Charter, which the barons forced from King John in 1215; next the Petition of Right in 1628, one of the conditions of which was that the king should not make "forced loans," that is, tax the people without their consent; third, the Habeas Corpus ("you may have the body") Act, which prevented the king from imprisoning a subject without due process of law; fourth, the Bill of Rights of 1689, and, fifth, the Act of Settlement of 1700, the last two still further limiting the power of the crown.

There were, of course, other grants, but the above are generally considered as the five great pillars of the English constitution. Now, the American colonists in 1765 considered themselves Britons, and therefore heirs to all the rights and privileges of this grand instrument, and they held that this act of the king and Parliament in taxing them without their consent was illegal and unconstitutional, and that they should resist it to the end; for if the king could lay this tax without their consent he could lay others and others, until their property was all swept away.

They were willing, they said, to pay their just share of the taxes, but if they did they must send men to Parliament to look after their rights and defend their interests. Such was the principle at stake.

Statesmen would have foreseen that the time had now come for making America a part of the empire and giving her due representation; but King George and his ministers were not statesmen, and they rushed blindly on to the disruption of their empire.

You have read in your histories how the other colonies resisted this act. New York's action was as spirited and determined as any. Hitherto her chief cause of complaint had been that she had not sufficient voice in her local government, and that the laws and regulations governing her trade were burdensome and intended to confine it solely to the mother country; but here was a clear case of the violation of an Englishman's constitutional rights, and her people determined to have nothing to do with the stamped paper.

The ship *Edward*, bearing the first cargo of it, arrived from England on October 23, 1765, and as she anchored under the guns of Fort George, though convoyed by a frigate and tender, she was greeted with hisses, derisive cheers, and menacing gestures by a great crowd of citizens gathered on the Battery to see her come in, while the shipping in the harbor lowered their flags to half-mast in token of grief. That night, men stealing by the rattle watch went quietly through the town, posting on trees, fences, and buildings handbills on which was written in a bold, free hand:

"PRO PATRICI.

"The first man that distributes or makes use of stamped paper let him take care of his house, person, and effects.
"VOX POPULI."

These handbills produced the effect designed. McEvers, the collector, to whom the stamped paper had been consigned, refused to touch it. No one could be found bold enough even to receive it into his warehouse or shop,

At last, in despair, Lieutenant Governor Colden ordered it stored in the fort until the 1st of November, the day the act was to go into operation, should arrive.

Thursday, the 31st of October, came, the day on which the governor was to take the oath that would put the act into effect. The city awoke in a fever of excitement. Bells were tolled; flags flew at half-mast. "The last day of liberty," the Whigs called it. Here and there muffled drums were heard beating the funeral march; great numbers of country people streamed in; there were, also, many sailors from the ships; the townspeople joined these, and all paraded the streets, singing patriotic songs, and threatening dire vengeance on any one daring to use the stamped paper. In the evening, two hundred of the principal merchants engaged in trade with England met in the assembly room of the City Arms Tavern, made brave and patriotic speeches, and passed spirited resolutions "to import no goods from England while the Stamp Act remained unrepealed," "to countermand all orders for spring goods already sent," "to sell no English goods on commission," and "to buy none from strangers that might be sent out."

At the same meeting a committee of correspondence was appointed to urge similar action on the part of other cities. Philadelphia merchants did not sign this "nonimportation agreement," as it was called, until the 14th, and Boston merchants not until December 9; so we see that both the nonimportation acts and the committees of correspondence of the Revolution, of which so much has been said, had their origin in New York.

Further, it was agreed at this time to hold a grand mass meeting next evening on the common (now City Hall Park). What took place then is so vividly described by a country lad, E. Carther by name, who came in with the others, that we give his letter just as it was written.

First he informed his parents what the governor did on this memorable Stamp Act day:

"He sent for the soldiers from Tortoise; he planted the cannon against the city; he fixed the cow horns with musket balls. Two cannon were planted against the fort gate for fear the mob should break in, loaded with grape shot; he ordered the cannon of the Battery to be spiked up for fear the mob should come so far as to break out in civil war and knock down the fort. Major James had said, 'Never fear, I will drive New York with 500 artillery soldiers.' He [Major James] placed soldiers at the Gaol to prevent the mob letting out the prisoners.

"He ordered 15 artillery soldiers at his house near the Coladge [Columbia College], where Black Sam formerly dwelt, and the rest of the soldiers he kept within the fort ready for an engagement."

In the evening the citizens began to muster about the streets.

"About seven in the evening I heard a great Hozaing near the Broadway. I ran that way with a number of others when the mob first began. They had an ephogy [effigy] of the Governor made of paper which sat on an old chair that a seaman carried on his head. The mob went from the Fields down the Fly [Pearl Street] Hozaing at every corner with amazing sight of candles. The mob went from there to Mr. McEvers who was appointed for Stamp master in London. Since he did not accept it they honored him with three cheers. From thence they went to the Fort that the Governor might see his ephogy if he dare show his face. The mob gave seven Hozas and threatened the officer upon the wall. They jeered Major James for saying he could drive New York with 500 men. The mob had assurance enough to break open the Governor's coach house, and took his coach from under the muzzles of his cannon. They put the eph-

ogy upon the coach, one sat up for coachman with the whip in his hand, whilst others drawed it about the town, down to the Coffee house, and the Merchants' Exchange."

After speeches by their leaders, they turned and marched back to the fort "with about 500 or 600 candles to alight them."

"I ran down to the fort to hear what they said. As the mob came down it made a beautiful appearance, and as soon as Major James saw them I heard him say from off the walls: 'Here they come by.'—As soon as the mob saw the fort they gave three cheers, and came down to it. They went under the cannon which was planted against them with grape shot. They bid a soldier upon the walls to tell the 'rebel drummer' or Major James to give orders to fire. They placed the gallows against the fort gate, and took clubs and beat against it, and then gave three Hozas in defiance. They then concluded to burn the ephogy, and the Governor's coach in the Bowling Green before their eyes."

After burning the coach, the people, mad with excitement, went to Major James's house and destroyed his furniture, except "one red silk curtain and the colors of the royal regiment," which they carried off in triumph.

Our letter writer continues: "The third day they was resolved to have the Governor dead or alive. The fort got up the fascines in order for battle, and the mob began before dark. The Governor sent for his Council which held about two hours whilst thousands stood by ready for the word. The Governor consented, and promised faithfully to have nothing to do with the stamps, and that he would send them back to London by Captain Davis of the *Edward*."

This account is in the main correct. At the people's demand the governor delivered the stamped paper to the mayor and aldermen, who deposited it in the City Hall, and no further attempt was made to enforce the odious tax in New York. The next spring, 1766, a new ministry, with the great statesman William Pitt at its head, came into power, and the obnoxious law was repealed, although Parliament still asserted its right to tax the colonies.

The Stamp Act served to separate men into two parties, and to give these body and form. From this time until the open rupture in 1775, they confronted each other in the city, the "Tory," "Royalist," or "ministerial" party, as it was variously called, on one side, and the "Whig," "patriot," or "rebel" party on the other. Each party had, of course, its leaders. First on the Royalist side was Lieutenant Governor Colden, who, until the newly appointed governor, Sir Henry Moore, should arrive, was clothed with supreme authority. Colden was eighty years of age at this time, a man of stanch loyalty, but stubborn, and lacking in tact and discernment. Next to him was General Thomas Gage, whom the Whig newspapers called irreverently "Tom Gage," the commander in chief of the British forces in America, whose large, double house stood on the present site of Nos. 67 and 69 Broadway. There was Major Thomas James, commander of the regiment of artillery and owner of the beautiful country seat "Vauxhall," on the banks of the Hudson near the foot of the present Chambers Street, and greatly disliked by the patriots for his arrogance and boastful threats. Other leaders were the Rev. Dr. Samuel Auchmuty, rector of Trinity Church; the Rev. Dr. Myles Cooper, president of King's College, later banished for his Tory sentiments and pamphlets; John Antill, postmaster; Daniel Horsmanden, chief justice of the province; Samuel Bayard, assistant secretary; Colonel William Bayard, the great merchant; John Harris Cruger, treasurer of the city; John Griffiths, master of the port; Thomas Buchanan, to whom later the tea ships were consigned; and many others, office-holders or those who received in some way largess from the king.

The patriots, on the other hand, were men without office or the hope of it, since their very acts disbarred them. Chief among them in boldness and energy was Isaac Sears, a merchant in the West India trade. John Lamb, an optician by trade, who later became a colonel in the Revolutionary army, was equally prominent. There was Alexander McDougall, a Scotchman by birth, and later a major general on the patriot side; John Morin Scott, an eminent lawyer; and Marinus Willett, who had marched with Abercrombie to Lake George and Ticonderoga, with Bradstreet to Fort Frontenac, and who later became a lieutenant colonel in the New York line, and in 1807 mayor of New York.

Sir Henry Moore arrived toward the close of 1765, and at once ordered a change of policy. He was a very different man from the acting governor, Colden, being bland, persuasive, soft-voiced, shrewd, and tactful. He "came as a friend among friends," he said, "and not to a revolted province;" and he gave orders to dismantle the fort and scatter the soldiers, while he set about healing the wounds his predecessor had made. Very soon a much better feeling existed, although the two parties still stood to their arms and kept a wary eye upon each other. An incident that occurred during the summer of 1766 impressed this forcibly on the governor's mind.

The Sons of Liberty, a patriotic society of the day, erected a "liberty pole" on June 4, 1766, the king's birthday, in honor of the repeal of the Stamp Act, and further celebrated the day with firing of cannon, a grand barbecue on the common, and bonfires in the evening. The flag that was later flung from the pole bore the words: "The King, Pitt, Liberty." Now, the repeal of

the Stamp Act had greatly angered the soldiers and Tories, who regarded it as a victory for the people, and this flag flaunting in their faces irritated them beyond endurance; they therefore determined to destroy it, and did so on the 10th of August by cutting down the pole itself. The Sons of Liberty raised it again, and again the soldiers leveled it. A third was quickly raised, and so close a watch kept upon it that it was not until the night of the 18th of March, 1767, that the soldiers succeeded in felling it. The patriots raised a fourth, and this time secured it with iron bands. The soldiers made two desperate attacks upon it, but were twice repulsed by the patriots, until at length, to keep the peace, Governor Moore interposed, and ordered the soldiers to cease their attempts. The latter now remained quiet until over three years had elapsed, and then one night sallied out against the pole, and cutting it down, piled the fragments against the door of Montague's Tavern, where the Sons of Liberty held their meetings.

This was adding insult to injury. The next day nearly the whole city, we are told, met on the common and passed resolutions " that all soldiers below the rank of orderly who appeared armed on the streets should be deemed disturbers of the peace, and be liable to arrest, together with all those found out of their barracks after roll call."

The soldiers met this by writing an insulting placard, which they posted throughout the city. Three of them were caught in the act by two stalwart Sons of Liberty, Isaac Sears and Walter Quackenbos, who attempted to take them as prisoners to the mayor's office, but were discovered by a party of soldiers from the lower barracks, who rushed to the rescue. But the Liberty Boys were also on the alert, and hurrying to the aid of their comrades, armed with canes, sticks, stones, bludgeons, and knives, a brisk battle was fought, in which the soldiers were worsted—not, however, until one patriot had been thrust through with a bayonet, and several others wounded. The next day, the soldiers, smarting under a sense of defeat, renewed the attack, first upon a woman who was going to market, then upon a party of sailors passing through the streets, one of whom, an old man, was stabbed with a bayonet and fell. Being driven off, they renewed the attack in the afternoon, and were again repulsed. This two days' battle with the military began January 18, 1770. The Boston massacre, in which it has been said the first blood spilled in the Revolution was shed, occurred March 5, 1770, or nearly two months later.

We have all read of the famous "Boston Tea Party" of December 16, 1773, following the duty laid upon tea by Parliament. New York had hers also, although it did not take place until some three months later, for the reason that the tea ship destined for New York was about three months overdue, having been driven out of her course by a storm. This first tea ship, the *Nancy*, was due in New York November 25, 1773, and the "Mohawks," an order similar to that which destroyed the tea in Boston, had made ready to receive her; at the same time the Sons of Liberty, which, under Governor Moore's pacific reign, had nearly died out, was revived and panoplied for the fray.

Sir William Tryon, a man of very different character, haughty, cruel, remorseless, had succeeded Moore in 1771, and by his words and manner quickly excited a feeling of resistance throughout the province. At last, on April 18, 1774, the long-expected tea ship was reported, and the Mohawks made ready to receive her. She had fallen in with a cyclone on the voyage, her captain, Lockyer, reported, had lost her mizzenmast and an anchor, sprung her maintopmast, and sustained other injuries. As "Holt's Journal" of April 21 said:

"Ever since her departure from Europe she has met

with a continued succession of misfortunes, having on board something worse than a Jonah, which, after being long tossed on the tempestuous ocean, it is hoped, like him, will be thrown back upon the place from whence it came. May it preach a lesson there as useful as the preaching of Jonah was to the Ninevites."

In this spirit the people received the tea which Parliament had decided to tax in order, as Lord North observed, " to try the question with America."

By agreement with the Sons of Liberty the New York pilots refused to bring the *Nancy* farther than Sandy Hook. There she was boarded by a committee of the Sons, who took possession of her boats, that her crew might not escape, and thus prevent her being sent back to England, which had been determined on. Lockyer consented to go back, and was allowed to come up to the city and see his consignee, but was not permitted to approach the customhouse, lest he should enter his vessel.

Before he could sail, however, the *London*, Captain Chambers, was reported. She, too, was boarded at Sandy Hook by the Liberty Boys; but as her captain positively declared he had no tea on board, he was allowed to come up to his dock. However, the committee had received private advices from Philadelphia that tea *was* on board, and as the *London* swung into her berth, about four in the afternoon, the whole committee boarded her and ordered the hatches opened, saying they were certain that she carried tea, and assuring Captain Chambers that they were ready to open every package in the cargo in order to find it; whereupon the captain, seeing concealment to be impossible, confessed that he had eighteen chests on board. Upon this the committee invited him to the great public room of Fraunces's Tavern to deliberate on the matter. They decided " to communicate the whole sense of the matter to the people, who were convened near the ship, which was accordingly done." The Mohawks were prepared to do their duty under cover of darkness, but the

Fraunces's Tavern.

people were so impatient that before night fell a number of them boarded the ship, took out the tea which was at hand, broke the cases, and emptied their contents into the river, without doing any harm to the ship or cargo. Several persons of reputation were placed below to keep tally, and about the companionway to prevent ill-disposed persons from going below the deck.

At ten o'clock the people all dispersed in good order, but in great wrath with the captain; and it was not without some risk of his life that he escaped.

By this time Captain Lockyer was able to fix the hour of departure for his return voyage; the people were informed of it and invited to meet on the dock whence he was to depart, and give him an idea of the feeling among them in regard to the taxed tea. He was to leave on Saturday morning at nine o'clock. "The bells will give notice about an hour before he embarks from Murray's Wharf," said the placards that were posted all over the city. As nine o'clock struck, the committee waited on him at his lodgings at the coffee-house, and escorted him to its balcony, that he might see the people and be seen by them. As he appeared, a band struck up "God Save the King," and the people raised a great shout. Then a procession was formed with the captain and committee at its head, and to the sound of martial music moved down Wall Street to Murray's Wharf, where a small sloop lay ready to take the captain to his ship down in the lower bay. The captain and the committee boarded this sloop. Captain Chambers, finding New York pretty warm for him, also took passage. Then the little craft spread sail and moved down harbor, while the city bells rang for joy, the ships in the port flaunted their gayest colors, the much-fought-for liberty pole on the common flamed with colors to its peak, and cannon planted at its base thundered forth the triumph of the people.

## XII. THE BATTLE OF LONG ISLAND.

NEW YORK was the theater of some important events in the War of the Revolution. On receiving news of the battle of Lexington four days after the event, Sunday, April 23, 1775, the patriot leaders warned the people, "who assembled, and not being able to secure the key of the arsenal [in the City Hall], where the colony's arms were kept, forced open the door and took six hundred muskets, with bayonets and cartridge boxes filled with ball cartridges." These arms were distributed among the more active citizens, who formed themselves into a volunteer corps and assumed the government of the city.

Bodies of men then went to the customhouse, demanded the keys, and took possession of the public stores contained therein. Next the patriots turned their attention to two vessels at the dock about to sail for Boston with supplies for General Gage's troops, Isaac Sears and John Lamb, with their Liberty Boys, boarding them, and speedily unloading the cargoes, valued at eighty thousand dollars. No resistance was offered by the garrison, which numbered but one hundred regulars, under command of Major Isaac Hamilton. Governor Tryon was in England. When Monday came and the merchants and artisans arrived at their shops and stores, they found the regular authority overturned and the city in the hands of the Sons of Liberty. All business was stopped; bodies of armed men patrolled the streets. In Paris, anarchy would have followed; but in New York eight days after the overthrow (May 1) the people quietly elected a committee of one hundred to govern them until the Continental Congress, which was soon to meet in Philadelphia, should constitute other authority.

There was a great demonstration when, on May 7, 1775, the delegates from Massachusetts and Connecticut passed through the city on their way to this Continental Congress at Philadelphia, and a second, on June 25, 1775, when Washington, the newly appointed commander in chief of the army, rode through on his way to take command of the forces investing Boston. By a strange coincidence Governor Tryon arrived the same evening from England, direct from personal interviews with the king and ministry.

Under the call of Congress for troops four regiments were raised in New York alone. A few small skirmishes occurred between them and the *Asia* and other British guard ships in the harbor, but New York saw no actual war until in July, 1776, Sir William Howe, with a large fleet and an army of veteran troops, arrived from Halifax to invest and capture the city. This was the same general and army, you will remember, that had been driven out of Boston by the Continentals the spring before, added to by new regiments from England. Washington and Putnam had been in New York all summer, fortifying. There was a cordon of earthworks across the lower part of the island, and there were barricades in the streets, and strong forts on Brooklyn and Columbia Heights, on the Long Island shore. The weakness of the position lay in the fact that the enemy, with his fleet, could ascend either the East River or the Hudson and cover the landing of his army with its guns. Howe, however, did not avail himself of this advantage, but landed his army at various points along the curving shores of Gravesend Bay, between Coney Island and the present Fort Hamilton, and attacked the American army, which Washington had advanced to defend Brooklyn Heights.

As the ground fought and marched over in the battle that ensued is all within the limits of the present borough of Brooklyn, it will be interesting to consider that battle in detail. No doubt you have ridden on your wheels through the pleasant shades of Prospect Park, or skimmed over the smooth surface of Flatbush Avenue to the rural hamlet of Flatlands, or taken the Ocean Parkway path to the sea, or Eighteenth Avenue, that runs to Bath Beach, or Fort Hamilton Avenue, skirting the southern border of Greenwood Cemetery, to Fort Hamilton; again, perhaps you have ridden out by the Eastern Boulevard and the roads leading from it eastward to the old Jamaica Plank Road, or from the terraced heights of Washington Park have looked down on the mighty city below,—if you have, you are familiar with the battle ground of August 27, 1776.

Let us see first where the American army was posted. If you draw a line straight across from the present Navy Yard to Gowanus Canal the region west and southwest

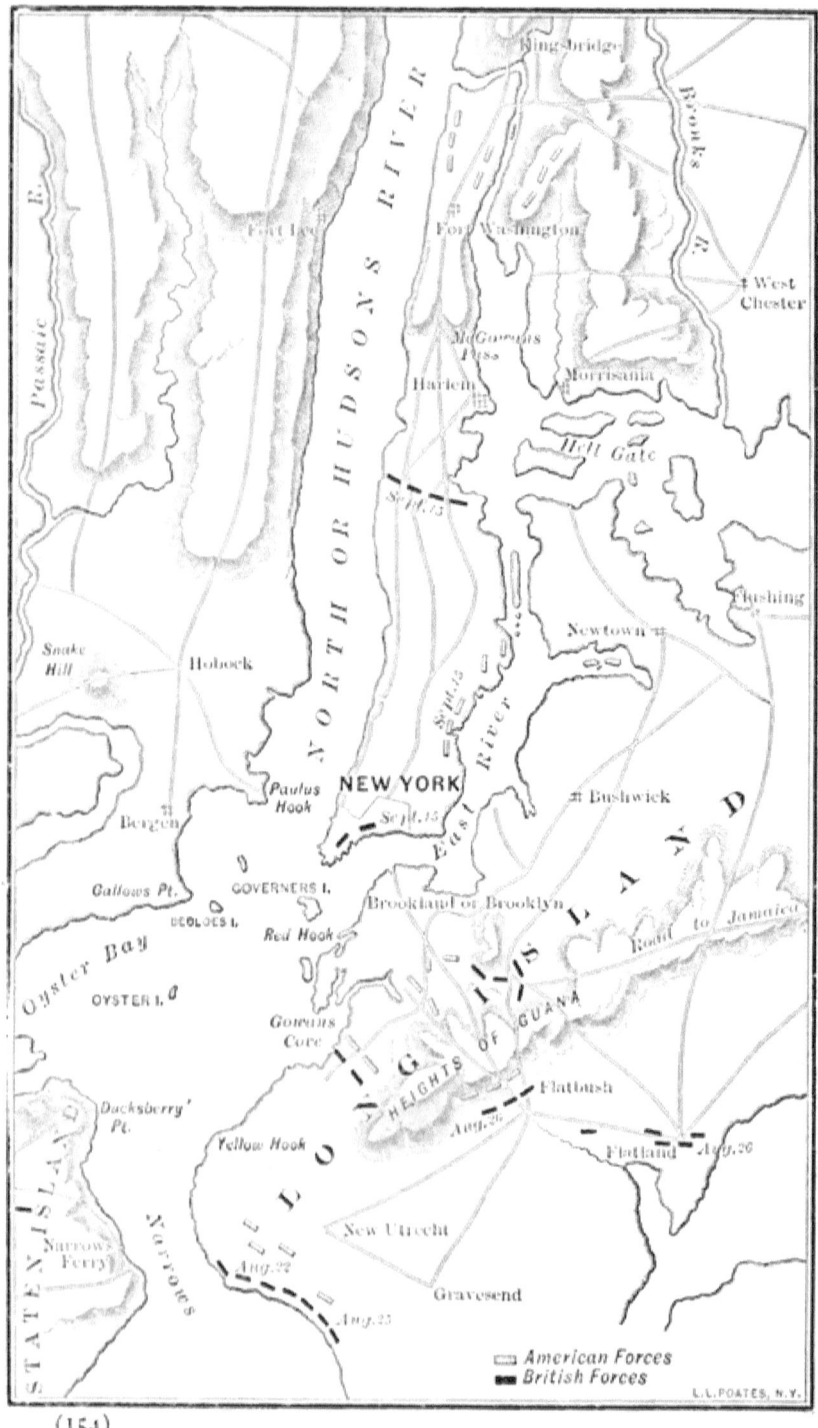

Plan of the Battle of Long Island.

is a peninsula ending in a sharp point called Red Hook, Gowanus Creek and marsh inclosing it on one side, and the Bay of the Wallabout on the other. The country then was mostly forest and farm. Gowanus Canal, now the center of business and trade, was then a sluggish creek flowing through a wide marsh. Columbia and Brooklyn Heights, the highest points in this peninsula, commanded New York, and on them General Lee and Lord Stirling had erected two forts, Stirling and the Citadel. When Putnam came he decided to throw a chain of forts, redoubts, and trenches from Gowanus Creek quite across the neck to the Wallabout. First, and nearest Gowanus, was Fort Box, on or near the present line of Pacific Street, a short distance above Bond. Next, and three hundred

Washington Park (Site of Fort Putnam).

yards west, was Fort Greene, star-shaped, mounting six guns, and lying between the present State and Schermerhorn streets. Still farther to the left was the "oblong redoubt," on the corner of the present De Kalb and Hudson avenues. Fort Putnam, star-shaped, mounting five guns, came next, its site still preserved in beautiful Washington Park. Below it, near the bay, was the "redoubt on the left," standing in the middle of the present Cumberland Street, between Willoughby Street and Myrtle Avenue.

If we take our station on the water tower near the main entrance to Prospect Park we can get a bird's-eye view of the whole battle ground. Before us, on the south, lies the "great plain," which in 1776 was covered with farm and forest, with three smiling villages on its bosom,—New Utrecht, Gravesend, and Flatbush,—whose position you can readily find on the map. The chain of hills, then called the Heights of Guana, which runs from the bay shore to East New York through Greenwood Cemetery and Prospect Park, was covered with dense forest and scrub impassable to an army. South Brooklyn was a swamp. Gowanus Creek showed great mills whose wheels were moved by the ebb and flow of the tides. Second, Third, and Fourth avenues were a morass, as was the whole region in that neighborhood, now covered with blocks of buildings.

At the north was the King's Highway, winding up the hill from Fulton Ferry, passing the Brooklyn church and hamlet, and continuing on, skirting the northern base of the hills, to Bedford and Jamaica. This road threw off branches leading to the villages in the plain—first, the

"Coast Road," which skirted the shore quite to the Narrows; second, the road to Flatbush, about a mile and a half beyond the American works; and, third, three quarters of a mile farther on, the road from Bedford to Flatbush. These roads reached the plain by gaps in the Heights of Guana, and were the only means by which an enemy in the plain could reach the American line, except that at the extreme left, four miles away, where the King's Highway passed through the range, was Jamaica Pass, at the present entrance to the Cemetery of the Evergreens.

On the Coast Road, hard by the Red Lion Tavern, a narrow lane called Martense Lane branched off to the left, and skirting the southern boundary line of the present Greenwood, connected with the roads on the plain. The Heights of Guana formed the American outer line of defense or skirmish line. The only one of the gaps defended by fieldworks was the Flatbush Pass, within the present limits of Prospect Park. This pass was defended by two batteries—a crescent-shaped redoubt that extended across the main street of Flatbush just within the village, and a smaller one at Valley Grove to guard the Port Road, which ran down to the East River along the present line of First Street.

Swarming like ants upon these fortifications, marching through the roads, drilling on parade, had been all summer perhaps the oddest, most incongruous army ever recruited since Falstaff's day. There were the green hunting shirts and leggings of the Marylanders, the dark-blue coats with red facings of the Delaware militia, the tow frocks and tarnished scarlet regimentals of the

Connecticut troops. There were the New Jersey riflemen, some in short red coats and striped trousers, some in blue coats, with leathern breeches ending in blue yarn stockings, and heavy shoes with brass buckles. Here was a Pennsylvania regiment in variegated costume: one company clad in brown coats faced with white and adorned with huge metal buttons; another showing blue coats faced with red; a third, brown coats faced with buff. Many from the backwoods wore fringed hunting shirts and leggings. Some marched and fought in their shirt sleeves.

The Virginians aroused envy by the superior quality of their uniform—white frocks adorned with ruffles at neck, wrists, and elbows, black, broad-brimmed slouch hats, black stocks, and hair in long queues. They were called the dandies of the army.

The arms of this impromptu host were quite as diverse and incongruous as its uniforms. There were the shotgun and old "king's arm" of the Puritans, the long "goose gun" of the New York Dutchmen, the musket of the Pennsylvanians, the deer-slaying rifles of the New Jersey, Maryland, and Virginia riflemen. Very few of them were furnished with bayonets or sufficient ammunition.

The total number of available men at Washington's command at this crisis was nineteen thousand, organized in five divisions, the division commanders being Putnam, Heath, Spencer, Sullivan, and Greene, with Knox commanding the artillery. Save Putnam and Spencer, these commanders had had very little military training; some of the subordinate officers were mere boys in years. Alexander Hamilton, later the greatest statesman of his time, who commanded a battery in Knox's division, was but nineteen. Aaron Burr, with whom his fate was later so interwoven, an aide on General Putnam's staff, was a youth of twenty, while Nicholas Fish, Brigadier General Scott's brigade major, was but eighteen.

A gallant and effective arm of the patriot force should be mentioned—the motley fleet of swift schooners, sloops, periaguas, row galleys, and whaleboats, commanded by Lieutenant Colonel Benjamin Tupper, which patrolled the harbor, rivers, and sound, and picked up deserters, spies, provision boats, and news of the enemy's movements with the greatest dispatch and impartiality.

When we consider the opposing army we wonder at the temerity of the patriots in attempting to oppose it. This army was composed mainly of regular soldiers—men trained to the profession of arms, veterans who had been under fire. There was Gage's Boston garrison, seasoned veterans from the West Indies, the Peninsula, Gibraltar, and other strongholds, Scotch who had won renown in a seven years' war, and Hessians whose trade it was to fight. Then the officers were men trained in the best military schools of Europe, lieutenant generals, major generals, brigadier generals—Howe and Clinton and Percy and Cornwallis, Mathews, Pigot, Grant, Robertson, Jones, Vaughan, Agnew, Leslie, Cleveland, Smith, and Erskine; in numbers there were twenty-three thousand Englishmen and eight thousand Hessians, thirty-one thousand men against the patriots' nineteen thousand; and besides this, a fleet of four hundred war ships and transports, among the former twenty frigates and ten ships of the line.

It was on the 29th of June that Lord Howe arrived. Nine days after, July 8, he threw nine thousand men ashore and occupied Staten Island. A few days later his brother, Admiral Howe, arrived with the rest of his forces—English regiments just sent out, and the Hessians whom King George had hired from the Landgrave of Hesse and other petty German rulers.

On the 12th of July the British frigates *Rose* and *Phœnix* ran past the batteries, and sailed up the Hudson as far as Haverstraw, to encourage the Tories of Westchester County and open communication with General Carleton, who was marching south from Canada by way of Lake Champlain to attack the Americans in the rear.

Lord Howe was a just and humane man, whose sympathies were with the Americans. He had been told by King George to offer pardon to all "rebels," as he termed them, who would submit. Howe, therefore, before offering battle, desired to meet the leaders and confer with them. Accordingly, on July 14, he sent an aide in a barge, with a letter addressed to "Mr. Washington." Tupper's alert whaleboats captured the barge in midharbor, and held it while they sent a messenger to headquarters to know if Washington would receive it. In reply General Knox and Colonel Reed, Washington's adjutant general, came down to confer with the officer.

He received them courteously. "I have a letter," said he, "for Mr. Washington." "We have no person of that name in our army," replied Colonel Reed.

"Will you not look at the address?" persisted the officer. "No, sir," replied Reed; "I cannot receive that letter." "I am sorry," said the envoy, and bowing, returned to the fleet.

Something more than personal vanity or military etiquette was involved here. For Howe to have addressed Washington as "General" would have been to acknowledge the authority of the Continental Congress, which had created him one. But this authority King George denied. According to his view, the Americans were simply rebellious subjects, liable by military usage and the law of nations to be summarily executed for treason if taken in arms.

For Washington, on the other hand, to have received the letter would have been to admit the king's contention.

A personal interview between Washington and Colonel Patterson, representing General Howe, was later arranged at the Kennedy mansion.

Colonel Patterson apologized for the address on the former letter, and produced another bearing the inscription, "George Washington, Esq., etc., etc., etc.," which, as it implied everything, General Howe hoped would be satisfactory. "True," replied Washington, "but it also implies anything;" and he declined to receive any letter not bearing his proper title. Colonel Patterson then said that the king desired to conciliate his American subjects and had given Lord Howe and his brother, Admiral Howe, power to offer pardon to all who would lay down their arms.

To this Washington replied that the Americans, having done no wrong, could accept no pardons. "They had but taken up arms to maintain their rights as Englishmen."

Finding his offers of peace spurned, Howe now proceeded to move against the American army by way of Long Island, although a large force was sent to attack Bergen, Elizabethport, and Perth Amboy, on the New Jersey shore. Twenty-four thousand men were detailed for the attack on Long Island.

On the night of August 22, 1776, the advance guard of this force landed on the shores of Gravesend Bay, between the present village of Bath Beach and Coney Island. At nine next morning four thousand light infantry crossed in flatboats from Staten Island, convoyed by the *Rainbow* and other men-of-war, and landed at what is now Fort Hamilton. An hour later a second division, of British and Hessians, entered boats, and rowing in regular ranks, landed at the bend of Gravesend Bay, at or near Bath Beach. Fifteen thousand men were ashore by noon, and spreading over Gravesend and New Utrecht plains under cover of the guns of the fleet.

Let us cross the East River with this boatload of soldiers which Washington is hurrying over to reënforce his brave fellows on the heights. The only means of propelling boats at this time, you remember, are oars and sails. Brooklyn Heights rise before us in their natural outlines, uncrowned by buildings. There is a village at the ferry, there are a few farmhouses on the slopes, and the two noble mansions of Phillip and Robert Livingston on Columbia Heights, but neither city nor town.

We will resume our stand on Reservoir Hill and view the position of the contending armies. The British hold the plain as far east as Flatbush and Flatlands. There are twenty-one thousand men there, for a third division of six thousand men has reënforced the fifteen thousand men that first landed. The Hessians and reserves are massed yonder at Flatbush, facing the pass, the main body, under Clinton and Percy, at Flatlands, two miles south, while Grant, with two brigades at Bath and New Utrecht, holds the Coast Road. The extreme right of the Americans, covering New Utrecht and the Martense Lane, is held by General Lord Stirling with his riflemen and Parsons's Connecticut troops. General Sullivan's division holds the center and extreme right, his regiments being stretched along the brow of the range for two miles on each side of the Flatbush Pass, and holding it. Meeting them on their left, Colonel Miles's Pennsylvania riflemen and some Connecticut levies take up the line and carry it east beyond Bedford Pass, but stop short of Jamaica Pass, leaving the latter unguarded—a grave mistake, by some charged to General Sullivan and by others to General Putnam. The whole number of American troops on this their outer line does not exceed twenty-eight hundred men, and in all there are barely eight thousand men, Washington not daring to leave his defenses on the New York side unmanned.

General Israel Putnam succeeded General Sullivan as commander in chief the day before, Washington remaining in New York. Putnam was a veteran of the French and Indian wars, a good fighter and strict disciplinarian, who had done excellent service at Bunker Hill a few months before. He, with the main body, held the inner or fortified line, whence it was thought he could quickly send aid to any part of the outer line when hard pressed.

The Tories promptly conveyed to Howe news that the Jamaica Pass had been left unguarded and was patrolled only by a few vedettes, and the latter's plan of battle was quickly formed, viz., to gain this pass quietly, march through it, turn the American left and gain the rear undetected, in which event the battle would be won. Grant, accordingly, was given orders to make a feint on Stirling on the morning of the 27th, at the Red Lion Tavern, a famous hostelry of that day, standing at the point where Martense Lane left the Coast Road, but by no means to bring on a serious battle until he should hear Clinton's guns in the American rear. De Heister and Knyphausen, commanding the Hessians, were given orders to attack Flatbush Pass at the same time, while Clinton and Percy were to steal around the American left with the entire right wing, gain Jamaica Pass, and double up the outer line on itself and the main body. This plan was carried out with perfect success.

At evening gun fire on the night of the 26th the troops of Clinton, Percy, and Cornwallis left their camp at Flatlands, with the fires still burning in order to deceive the Americans, and began their march "across the country through the new lots toward Jamaica Pass," as Lord Howe wrote in his report.

At the front were three Flatbush Tories as guides; then came Clinton with the light dragoons and a brigade of light infantry ; then Cornwallis and the reserves, with fourteen pieces of light artillery ; then Lords Howe and Percy. This force toiled on in the darkness along the sandy road from Flatlands as far as Shoemakers Creek, and then, the better to escape detection, crossed over through the fields to the Jamaica Road, striking it at William Howard's Halfway House, a few yards southeast of the pass.

Leaving his main army in the fields, Howe, with his aids and a small bodyguard, went forward, and the former, with a civilian's hat on and a camlet cloak drawn over his uniform, entered the tavern and ordered a drink.

"Have you joined the association?" he asked of the tavernkeeper.

"Yes," replied Howard.

"That's all very well; stick to your colors; but now you are my prisoner and must lead me across these hills, out of the way of the rebels, the nearest way to Gowanus," was the reply.

Howard led them around the pass by a bridle path that traversed what is now Evergreen Cemetery, and gained the Jamaica Road in the rear of the pass. They found the pass unguarded, and at once sent word to Clinton to hurry forward with the main body, which had been left in the fields, and occupy it.

But where was the vedette that had been set to patrol the pass? On this particular night it consisted of five young American officers of undoubted bravery and patriotism, who had volunteered for the perilous work —Van Wagener (one of the heroes of Quebec), Troup, Dunscomb, Hoogland, and Gilliland. Their orders were to patrol the pass and send news of the advance of the foe. But they erred from excess of zeal: not dreaming that the enemy would advance through the fields, they went forward on the road, the quicker to discover a possible advance, and the British slipped in between and captured them.

The young men were at once hurried into the presence of Clinton, who questioned them closely as to the troops, the forts, and the positions of the Americans; but they refused to answer.

"Under other circumstances," said Dunscomb, "you would not dare insult us in this manner."

Clinton, angered, called him an "impudent rebel," and threatened to hang him.

"No, you will not," replied Dunscomb, "for Washington can hang man for man."

The army now took breakfast and then hurried on down the King's Highway to Bedford, where they arrived about half-past eight in the morning. At this point they were well in the rear of the American outer line, about half a mile distant from it, and a mile and a half from Putnam's position. They could hear the thunder of De Heister's guns, now hotly engaged with Sullivan for possession of the Flatbush Pass.

In a short time they were discovered by Miles, who now found himself attacked by them in the rear, while cannonading down near the Red Lion Tavern told that Grant had obeyed orders and was engaging Stirling in that quarter.

The patriots saw that they were caught in a trap, between two fires, and cut off from their supports. A terrible hand-to-hand conflict of two hours now ensued in the woods and thickets, between Miles's and Sullivan's men on the one side and the British and Hessians, who, as we have seen, had penned them up between them— a fight with bayonet and sword and clubbed musket and branches rent from the trees; a struggle to the death, no quarter being asked or given. No supports were sent them by Putnam, for he knew not where to send, his whole line being engaged. The unequal combat could not long continue, however, and about noon Sullivan's and Miles's men broke and fled into the woods. A few gained the fortified line, but most of them were killed or taken prisoners.

Meantime the honors of the day had been won by Stirling, Parsons, and the sturdy troops of the Connecticut, Delaware, and Maryland lines.

On the night before the attack, August 26, Grant advanced by both the Coast Road and Martense Lane as ordered, and by midnight reached the vicinity of the Red Lion Tavern, where he came upon a guard of Americans under Major Bird, who at once sent word to Putnam. The latter ordered Stirling to check them, and that general, placing himself at the head of Haslet's Delaware battalion and Smallwood's Maryland regiment, hurried to the spot, closely followed by General Parsons, with Hunt's Connecticut regiment of two hundred and fifty men. A full half mile this side of the Red Lion Tavern they met Colonel Atlee's regiment retiring before the British column, whose front could be seen in the dim light of the dawn, a little in advance of the present entrance to Greenwood. Grant now formed line of battle across the Coast Road (in the vicinity of the present Thirty-eighth and Thirty-ninth streets, between Second and Third avenues), from the marsh on the east to the crest of the hills that now form the western boundary of Greenwood.

Stirling took post on the slopes of the hills between Eighteenth and Twentieth streets, a little to the northwest of the present Battle Hill in Greenwood, a company of riflemen being posted on the edge of the woods and along a ledge at the foot of the hill. A number of the latter climbed the trees, and from that coign of vantage picked off the British officers as they advanced. One huge Marylander was seen to kill Major Grant and another officer in this way, when he was discovered, and a whole platoon was ordered to advance and fire into the tree; at its fire he fell to the ground, pierced by a dozen bullets.

A Maryland regiment was posted on a low, wooded hill beside the Coast Road, at about the foot of the present Twenty-third Street. Here, awaiting attack, Stirling made a stirring address to his troops, reminding them that a few months before he had heard this same Major Grant openly boast in the British Parliament that the Americans could not fight, and that with five thousand men " he could march from one end of the continent to the other."

Pointing to the head of Gravesend Bay, he continued: " Grant may have his five thousand men now; we are not so many, but I think we are enough to prevent his getting farther than that mill pond."

In reality Grant had seven thousand men, Stirling sixteen hundred.

For two hours the grim lines faced each other, Grant, as we have seen, having positive orders not to force a battle until he heard the guns of the flanking column in the American rear.

About ten he heard them, and began pushing Stirling harder. Eleven o'clock, half-past eleven, came, and still Stirling had no orders to retreat, although he judged from the firing that the enemy was rapidly gaining his rear. This was the fact. Clinton and the Hessians together, as we have seen, had beaten back Sullivan and Miles, gained the passes, and by noon had carried the pursuit up to the walls of Fort Putnam, which they could have carried by assault, no doubt, had they attempted it. The men were eager for it, but Howe would not consent.

Meantime Cornwallis, with a heavy column, had been detached, and was pushing down the Port Road toward the East River, at first on the left and then in the rear of Stirling's long, thin line.

Washington remained in New York until he saw that the city was not to be attacked, then crossed to Brooklyn, and from the heights saw that Stirling had been surrounded and was in danger of being cut to pieces. He could not send relief without weakening his main line, and with anxiety that may be imagined watched that brave leader extricate himself. The latter saw that his only hope of escape was to drive Cornwallis's advance back along the Port Road toward Flatbush, until he could get between it and Fort Box, and escape under cover of its guns across Brower's milldam. Therefore, leaving his main body, under Parsons, fiercely engaged with **Grant**, he placed himself at the head of Smallwood's riflemen, and moved along the Gowanus Road in the face of a hail of fire from cannon, rifles, and muskets, pushing the enemy back till they rallied and stood firm under cover of the old stone Cortelyou house, the same which had sheltered the Labadist travelers over a hundred years before. This they would have carried, no doubt, had not the British wheeled two guns into position before them and mowed the attacking column down with grape and canister. Three times the brave fellows charged the house, once driving the gunners from their pieces within its shadow.

"Good God!" cried Washington, watching from his hilltop. "What brave fellows I must this day lose!"

The odds were too great, however, and at last the depleted column took refuge in a cornfield, where some surrendered, some were bayoneted, and a few made their escape by swimming Gowanus Creek. Stirling fled over the hills and yielded up his sword to De Heister, the Hessian commander, scorning to deliver it to the British. Meantime Parsons, on Battle Hill, had made a gallant stand, but his position was at last carried, and many of his men captured. Some of them escaped across the marsh. He succeeded in hiding himself in a swamp, and thence escaped to the American lines. This ended the battle of Brooklyn Heights. Of the five thousand Americans engaged, nearly half were killed, wounded, or prisoners.

Howe did not at once attack the line of forts, though they were defended now by scarcely three thousand men. His artillery was not up, he lacked axes for cutting palisades, scaling ladders and the like, so he sat down for a siege by regular approaches.

You may be sure that it was an anxious time for Washington and the other patriot leaders. More troops were ordered over from New York. Fortunately, next day it rained heavily, and the British contented themselves with a brisk cannonade and with sending out skirmishing parties. At evening they broke ground for intrenchments within five hundred yards of the American line, and that night threw up a redoubt just east of Fort Putnam, from which they opened fire on that fort.

Next day, the 29th, a dense fog hung over water and heights, veiling everything. News soon came that part of the British fleet had passed round the island and was now in Flushing Bay, on the north shore. This led Washington at five o'clock to call a council of his officers to decide whether to retreat or to fight. They decided to retreat.

The American army was in evil plight. If the enemy's fleet should sail up and hold the East River it would cut off its line of retreat. (The fleet would have done this on the battle day, we know now, but for lack of a wind.) The loss in men and officers on the 27th had disorganized the army. The men were wearied with constant watching and alarms. Their ammunition had been largely spoiled by the incessant rains of the last two days. Lastly, Howe was raising his trenches against them and would soon order an assault.

All through that eventful day Washington had been making secret preparations for a retreat. He had sent Colonel Trumbull to Assistant Quartermaster Hughes in

New York, with orders to impress at once craft of every description, from Spuyten Duyvil to Hell Gate, and have them in the "east harbor" by dark. Orders were sent also to General Heath, commanding at Kingsbridge, to seize all boats in his district and man them with the Salem and Marblehead fishermen of his command. It was given out that the boats would be used to ferry over certain New Jersey troops who were to relieve those on the heights. In the general orders to the army issued at the same time a similar fiction was employed, a retreat not being mentioned. The regiments were to be relieved by fresh New Jersey militia, and were commanded to be in marching order by nightfall, knapsack on back, and muskets and camp equipage in hand.

By dark a nondescript fleet had been collected at the Fulton Ferry dock—sloops, sailboats, galleys, periaguas, scows, rowboats, whaleboats—everything afloat, and with the hardy fishermen of Cape Ann and Cape Cod in command of them. In this retreat Washington deceived the British as completely as the latter had deceived him on the morning of the 27th. Leaving their camp fires brightly burning, silently as ghosts the grim ranks marched to the ferry through mud and darkness, Hitchcock's Rhode Islanders first, and then regiment after regiment, until by dawn all were across the river except General Mifflin's six regiments, which had been left to hold the redoubts.

Through all the hours of that long, dark night detection would have meant ruin. But how were the gallant Mifflin and his men to be drawn off without attracting attention? The same kind Providence which, by withholding the wind, had prevented the enemy's frigates from ascending and holding the river, again interposed. Heavy masses of dense fog rolled up from the bay and covered the frowning heights with a gray curtain. Mifflin retired under its cover. As the last outpost stole away it heard the sound of pickax and shovel busily plied in the British trenches. Before 7 A. M. the entire force was on the New York shore. When Howe awoke that morning he found that an army of nine thousand men, with stores, baggage, and artillery, had been spirited away while he slept. Some one has said that "to conduct a skillful retreat is equal to winning a great victory."

## XIII. THE BATTLE OF HARLEM HEIGHTS.

THE 30th and 31st of August, 1776, were anxious days in New York. Tents, arms, clothes, baggage, ammunition, all manner of camp equipage, soaked with rain, obstructed the streets and sidewalks; squads of soldiers off duty wandered wearily about or lingered on the corners. In the defenses—McDougall's and the Oyster batteries on a little hill in the rear of Trinity Church, Fort George and the Grand Battery in the present Battery Park, Whitehall Redoubt at the foot of the present Whitehall Street, Waterbury's on the dock at the angle of Catherine and Cherry streets, Badlam's between Madison and Monroe streets, and Spencer's between Clinton and Montgomery—the gunners stood at attention, for all expected an immediate attack. Why it was not made is one of several puzzling things connected with this whole defense of New York.

Why, in the first place, in view of the vastly greater force of his enemy, both by land and sea, did Washington attempt to hold New York at all? The final result could not have been in doubt; but if he was resolved to fight, why did he not seize and fortify Harlem Heights, including McGowans Pass, and thus keep open his line of retreat? And why, on the other hand, did Howe wait four full days after landing on the Gravesend plain before marching against the Americans, thus giving them time to prepare for battle? And why, after his victory of August 27 with his superior force, did he not assault the patriots' line? And why did he not ascend the Hudson with his fleet and seize the undefended Harlem Heights, thus cutting off Washington's line of retreat and compelling him to surrender his whole army?

Washington probably decided to hold New York because he feared the effect on the country and on the world of yielding the city without a struggle. This was really the second battle of the war. It had been said that his ragged Continentals would not stand in open battle against the seasoned veterans of Europe,

and he wished to prove the contrary. Again, our envoys to France were even then at the court of the French king, seeking the alliance which was soon declared, and which the bravery of the heroes of Battle Hill and Mount Prospect may have hastened. As for Lord Howe's acts, we have no explanation for them except that he was in sympathy with the Americans and wished to aid their cause.

New York in 1776 was a town of twenty-five thou-

Fort at McGowans Pass.

sand people and four thousand houses, filling the apex of the acute angle made by the two rivers, thus—V. Most of the town lay below the present Chambers Street, and comprised an area of less than one square mile. But one road led off the island, the Kingsbridge or "Boston Post Road," which left Broadway at the present post office building, followed Chatham Street to the present Chatham Square, thence the Bowery and Fourth

Avenue to Fourteenth Street, crossed Union Square northwest, thence followed the present line of Broadway to Madison Square, then turned northeast and ran on between Fourth and Second avenues to Fifty-third Street, there took a more easterly course to Ninety-second Street, where it turned west and entered the present Central Park, and continued therein until it had threaded a narrow defile called McGowans Pass, from the fact that the farmhouse of a man of that name was situated there. From this pass, which was about on the line of One Hundred and Seventh Street, the road followed over Harlem Lane, and crossed the Harlem River by a small wooden bridge called the King's bridge. This was the only route by which Washington's army could gain the high ground on the opposite shore.

There was another road on the western side of the island, the "Bloomingdale Road," which left the Post Road at about the present corner of Twenty-third Street and Fifth Avenue, and passed through the hamlet of Bloomingdale to the farmhouse of Adriaen Hoofland, at about One Hundred and Eighth Street, where it ended abruptly. Still another road ran from the upper part of the city to the village of Greenwich on the Hudson, at about the foot of the present Fourteenth Street, and then continued as a pretty rustic lane until it joined the Bloomingdale Road at Forty-third Street. The whole island above Fourteenth Street was a mass of crag, forest, swampy thicket, and natural meadow.

With Brooklyn Heights in possession of the enemy, the question arose whether to defend New York or burn it and retreat to the Highlands of the Hudson. Washington referred it to Congress, and that body gave him sole discretion in the matter. He accordingly called a council of his officers on September 12, at which it was decided to evacuate the city; without destroying it, however, as it was thought that it might soon be recovered.

It was quite time, for the British commander was already moving his troops with a view of attacking the city. On September 3 the frigate *Rose* had sailed up the East River past the Battery, conveying thirty whale-boats to be used in crossing the river. On the 12th, thirty-six more boats passed up, and on the 14th four frigates and six transports joined the *Rose*.

Washington now pressed all his teams and transports into the work of removing the sick, wounded, and stores

Apthorpe Mansion.

to Kingsbridge. One more day would have completed the task; but on the morning of the 15th of September the British moved on the city, and that same afternoon captured it. Washington, the night before, had left New York and fixed his headquarters at the Apthorpe mansion, which stood on the Bloomingdale Road, at the corner of what is now Ninth Avenue and Ninety-first Street. Putnam's and Sullivan's divisions garrisoned the city and the forts; Scott's New York brigade was stationed on the Stuyvesant estate, about on the line of the present East Fifteenth Street; Wadsworth, with his Connecticut troops, was at Twenty-third Street; and Douglas, with three regiments of Connecticut militia, was at Kips Bay, at the foot of the present Thirty-fourth Street.

This was the situation on Sunday morning, September 15. Soon after daybreak Douglas, at Kips Bay, saw five frigates move up the river and come to abreast of his position. At the same time, from the mouth of Newtown Creek, on the opposite shore, issued eighty-four row galleys filled with grenadiers in scarlet uniforms, looking, as a soldier aptly said, "like a clover field in full bloom." The grenadiers with their oars urged the boats on. As they neared the shore, all at once, with a burst of thunder, the seventy-five guns of the frigates belched a storm of grapeshot on the devoted patriots. One soldier thought "his head would go with the sound;" "but," he added, "we kept the line until they were almost leveled upon us, when the officers, seeing we were exposed to the rake of their guns, gave the order to leave."

At the same time the galleys were beached a little to the left, and the grenadiers leaped ashore without opposition. All the American brigades along the river now began to retreat northward toward Kingsbridge, over which ran, as we have said, the only road leading at that time from the island. But the British pursued them so hotly that they were soon in panic-stricken flight. Up the Post Road they ran, every man for himself, Douglas, Huntington, and Prescott in vain trying to check and reform them.

Washington, at the Apthorpe house, heard the firing, leaped to his horse, and spurred down the Bloomingdale Road and across by a country lane to the Post Road, reaching it just as the mob of frightened fugitives came toiling and panting up, some taking to the fields in their panic, some keeping to the road. As it happened, Parsons's and Fellows's brigades, which had been ordered up to check the rout, appeared at this moment, and Washington shouted to them, "Take to the walls, take to the cornfield!"

The men did so, but the enemy's vanguard appearing at this critical instant on the brow of the hill, they broke and fled in as much disorder as the militia. Washington, at the sight, is said to have lost his usual self-command, and to have dashed in among the fugitives, waving his hat and imploring them to make a stand; but it was useless, and recognizing this at last, he commanded the retreat to be continued, while he spurred on to Harlem Heights to make preparations to receive the British there.

Meantime, what of Putnam's division, which was garrisoning the forts in the lower part of the city? At the first sound of the guns it had been put in retreat toward Harlem, following the Bloomingdale Road, while Knox's artillery and Silliman's brigade of infantry took post at Bayards Hill Fort, on a bluff at about the present corner of Grand and Mulberry streets, to cover its retreat. This was perhaps two hours before the rout at Murrays Hill, and the column, though moving slowly, was now well up the island. Putnam, finding himself unable to rally the fugitives on the Post Road, next turned his attention to his own column, first ordering his aid, Major Aaron Burr, with a company of dragoons, to bring off Knox's and Silliman's brigades at Bayards Hill—an order very successfully carried out by Major Burr, who first led the brigades to the main column, and then by lanes and devious ways past the British advance, which by this time had gained the center of the island, until they rejoined the main body in Harlem.

The army was now out of the city. Harlem Heights had become the seat of war.

If we visit the great brown cliff now known as Morningside Park, and take our stand at about where One Hundred and Nineteenth Street crosses it, we can take in the battlefield at a glance. At our feet the plain of Harlem, now covered with brick and stone, stretches away to the east. North, directly across the valley, rises another rocky height, known in 1776 as Point of Rocks, and extending thence northwest in a series of points and ledges to the Hudson, the whole range being known as Harlem Heights. Washington massed his army on the Point of Rocks after the retreat, fixing his headquarters in the Morris house (now the Jumel mansion), which still stands in its grounds a little southwest of High

Jumel Mansion.

Bridge. The British took post where we are supposed to stand. The plain below, then mostly covered with forest, was the scene of the battle of Harlem Heights.

It was the aim of the British to drive the Americans from their position. The latter, however, did not stand on the defensive, but descended into the plain and brought on the battle. Washington at daylight on the morning of the 16th of September dispatched Colonel Thomas Knowlton, with a small force, to beat up the forests along the bank of the Hudson, and see what the British were doing. Knowlton did so, found the enemy at the base of the cliffs, and after exchanging shots retreated, drawing a force of some three hundred men in pursuit. On hearing the firing Washington sent his adjutant general, Colonel Reed, to learn the cause, and on the latter's reporting that Knowlton was retreating before a superior force, sent forward reënforcements which quickly put the British to flight.

The second or main battle began at ten o'clock in the morning and lasted till two, ending in the defeat of the British.

About ten a squadron of British cavalry appeared in the plain, and blew their bugles in the face of the Americans as at a fox hunt. Washington accepted the challenge and ordered Major Leitch, with his Virginian riflemen, and Colonel Knowlton, with his Connecticut rangers, to gain the rear of the British by their right flank, while the main body attacked them in front. At the sound of firing the enemy hurried up his reserves. Unfortunately, the riflemen and rangers, losing their way in the forest, struck the right flank of the British instead of their rear, as ordered, which alarmed the English commander, and he ordered up his choicest regiments. Washington responded by sending in detachments of Douglas's, Nixon's, Richardson's, and Griffeths's regiments, the same troops that had fled so ingloriously the day before, and the battle in the plain opened with spirit. But to-day these same troops fought like veterans and forced the British back upon their reserves on the hilltop. Knowlton and Leitch, on their side of the field, were equally successful, and rolled the British left back upon the heights. There the combined forces made a stubborn stand, but at last were driven from the cliffs as they had been from the valley. About noon, meeting with reënforcements in their retreat, they made a fresh stand in a buckwheat field, and held their ground for about two hours, but were finally routed again and chased for two miles, the Americans mocking their bugles as they pursued. The patriots had won a barren victory, however, except that it had blotted out the disgrace of the day before and renewed their courage and confidence in themselves; for Howe remained master of New York, and could, by seizing Washington's line of retreat across the Harlem, hem him in and force him to surrender.

The Americans continued to hold Fort Washington (which stood on the high point of land south of Spuyten Duyvil, at what would be the intersection of Fort Washington Avenue and One Hundred and Eighty-third Street, if cut through),[1] with half a score of supporting forts and three lines of intrenchments extending from the Hudson to the Harlem, until the morning of November 16, 1776, when they were attacked by a force of eighty-nine hundred British and Hessians under the immediate command of Lord Howe himself. After a gallant and desperate defense of two hours, the British threw a detachment across the Harlem below the second line of intrenchments and assailed the Americans in the rear; and a concerted attack being made in front and on both flanks at the same time, Colonel Robert Magaw, the officer in command, surrendered his entire force.

---

[1] James Gordon Bennett's house stands on or near the site of the north bastion.

It was the most serious reverse the Americans had yet met. Some three thousand men, the flower of the American army, were captured, with forty-three guns and a large amount of stores. The British loss was seventy-eight killed and three hundred and eighty wounded, the American, fifty-four killed and twelve wounded.

## XIV. NEW YORK IN THE GRASP OF THE INVADER.

WHEN Howe's army assumed control of New York, September 16, 1776, she bore much the appearance of a dismantled city. Many of the people had fled, taking with them everything they could carry. Houses and stores were closed, churches and public buildings barred; even the bells had been removed from the belfries. The city remained in captivity during the whole period of the war. At midnight on September 21, 1776, five days after Howe took possession, a fire broke out in a low groggery near Whitehall Street, and, fanned by a strong south wind, swept like a prairie fire through the city. Nearly every building as far north as King's College, including Trinity Church, its rectory and charity school, and the Lutheran church, was destroyed. Four hundred and ninety-three houses and several churches were burned. The British jumped to the conclusion that the torch had been applied by the Americans to prevent their using the city for winter quarters, and Howe so charged in his official report; but this the patriot leaders indignantly denied. "By what means it happened we do not know," wrote Washington to Governor Trumbull the day after the fire, and Colonel Reed wrote to his wife the same day:

"There was a resolve in Congress against our injuring it, so that we neither set it on fire, nor made any preparations for the purpose." Much suffering was experienced by the poor people thus deprived of their homes.

Following close on the heels of the fire came one of the most tragical incidents of the Revolution—the execution of Captain Nathan Hale of Connecticut as a spy. This gallant young officer, barely twenty-one, a graduate of Yale College, and about to be married to a beautiful girl, at Washington's request had volunteered to enter the British lines and gain intelligence of Howe's numbers, position, and plans. Disguised as a wandering schoolmaster, he succeeded, and had on his return nearly regained his whaleboat at Huntington, when he was captured by a yawl from a British frigate lying near by, and sent to New York as "a prisoner taken within the lines," that is, as a spy.

He had known before venturing what his fate would be if taken— death by hanging. Howe called a court martial for the next day to try him, but Hale told them he would save them the trouble, and boldly avowed himself a spy in the service of General Washington. The board thereupon condemned him to be hanged the next day, which was Sunday. Hale met his fate with a lofty patriotism which has rendered him immortal. As he stood upon a cart under an apple tree in the

Nathan Hale.

Rutgers orchard, with the noose about his neck, one of his enemies said tauntingly, "This is a fine death for a soldier." "Sir," replied Hale, "there is no death which would not be rendered noble in such a glorious cause." His last words have become a heritage of the race. "I only regret," said he, "that I have but one life to lose for my country."

For seven years martial law governed the city. New York became the headquarters of the British army, its storehouse and hospital, and the prison of those Americans unfortunate enough to be taken in arms. In the battles at the time of its capture it is estimated that five thousand prisoners were taken. The usual prisons could not accommodate them, and so the French church, the Brick, Middle Dutch, and North Dutch churches were seized and turned into prisons. Besides these King's College, the sugarhouse on Liberty Street, the new jail, the Bridewell, and the old City Hall were also used. As the war progressed and more captives were taken, old ships condemned for unseaworthiness were moored in the East River and used for prisons. The sufferings of the poor prisoners confined in them were terrible, and thousands died.

In Liberty Street, just south of the Middle Dutch Church, stood within the memory of men now living a heavy, gloomy stone building, five stories high, with small, deep windows rising tier above tier like portholes in a ship of the line. Each of its five floors was divided into two bare, dungeonlike apartments, on the walls of which might be traced the names of prisoners carved there nearly a century before.

This was the old sugarhouse of the Livingstons, the prison of most ominous fame of any of the Revolution. A strong oaken door opened on Liberty Street, and another on the southeast gave access to a damp, vermin-infested cellar. While held as a prison two sentinels were constantly on guard to prevent the escape of the desperate captives. Truly they who entered here left hope behind, like the wretches whom Dante saw crossing the portals of the inferno.

"In the suffocating heat of summer,"

The Livingston Sugarhouse.

wrote William Dunlap, "I saw every narrow aperture of those stone walls filled with human heads, face above face, seeking a portion of the external air." "Seats there were none," testified another eyewitness, "and their beds were but straw intermixed with vermin. For many weeks the dead cart visited the prison every morning, into which eight and ten corpses were flung, piled up like sticks of wood, and then dumped into ditches in the outskirts of the city."

The prison ships were even worse, if we may believe the tales told of them. They were at first assigned to prisoners taken on the high seas, but later confined landsmen as well. The principal ships were the *Jersey*,

*Whitby, Good Hope, Scorpion, Falmouth, Prince of Wales, Hunter,* and *Strombolo.* Of the *Jersey* the more fearful tales were told, perhaps because in her more were confined and more died in their bonds. It has been asserted that 10,644 prisoners, the flower of American manhood, died in her during the war, and were buried on the adjoining Brooklyn shore. Her position was in the little bay known as the Wallabout, now the Navy Yard.

The prisoner newly committed to her fever-infected hold was brought on board, his name and rank taken, his weapons and money, if he had any, removed, and he was then ordered below, where he found a thousand wretched beings racked with disease and emaciated with hunger. He was at once assigned to a "mess" of six men, and every morning, as the steward's bell sounded, formed in line, and received his daily ration of biscuit, peas, beef or pork. On some days flour, suet, oatmeal, and butter were added to this bill of fare, but never fresh vegetables. "The peas," said a survivor, "were damaged, the butter rancid, the biscuit moldy and often full of worms, the flour sour, the beef and pork unsavory. Not so much the fault of the king as of his rapacious commissioners, who exchanged good provisions for bad, and by curtailing rations and by other expedients heaped up large fortunes at the expense of the prisoners."

The suffering and mortality here are not to be ascribed so much to the British government as to the petty officers placed over the prisoners, who not only robbed them, but took a brutal delight in torturing them and adding to their discomforts in every way possible.

When morning came, the hatches were removed, the poor prisoners brought up their beds and spread them on the deck to air, washed down the floors, and spent the day on deck. At sunset the guards would cry, "Down, rebels, down!" The hatches were then put in place and fastened, and the captives stretched themselves in rows to sleep in the stifling, feverish air. If one died, his fellows sewed the body in his blanket; it was lowered into a boat, which was rowed ashore by the guard, and the body buried in a shallow trench.

There were many escapes. For instance, on a stormy night in 1779, nine sea captains and two pirates overpowered the guard and escaped in the ship's boat. The following winter fifteen prisoners gained their freedom by walking on the ice, that formed sufficiently hard to bear them.

New York was not a very pleasant place to live in during these seven years of war. Martial law prevailed; that is, there was no law but the will of the commander in chief. Any citizen might on suspicion be seized by the brutal provost guard and sent to prison, to be tried by a military court.

The burnt district (added to by another great fire in August, 1778) was soon covered by a nondescript array of tents and shanties that housed the scum and refuse of the British army—desperate villains, insomuch that respectable citizens were afraid to venture into the streets after dark. The people, too, were in constant fear of an attack by the Americans. All the adherents of the patriot cause who could left the city. On the other hand, many Tories whom the Americans had driven from the country fled hither for protection. Business was largely suspended.

It is doubtful if any but the Tories were sad when the news of peace came and the British prepared to leave the city. The 25th of November, 1783, was appointed for this happy event. At an early hour the rear guard of the British army embarked at the Battery and pulled away to their ships. At the same time the Continentals marched down from the Bowery with drums beating and standards waving in the breeze.

When the head of the column reached Cope's Tavern, at the corner of Broadway and Rector Street, it halted to receive a civic procession that had started from the Bull's Head Tavern, in the Bowery, about the same time. In this procession marched most of the notables, civil and military, of the day.

Captain Delevan's Westchester Light Horse led the advance. Next came General Washington, and George Clinton, governor of New York, with their suites, on horseback; next the lieutenant governor and members of the city council for the time being, four abreast; then the generals of the army,—Knox, Steuben, McDougall, James Clinton, and others,—eight abreast; then citizens on horseback; next the Speaker of the Assembly, and after him a great body of citizens on foot. When the head of this procession halted before Cope's Tavern, the soldiers presented arms, the drums beat, the people cheered, and the guns of Fort George thundered a salute. Addresses were then made to the general and the governor by prominent citizens, and in the evening there was a grand banquet at Fraunces's Tavern. Thus New York welcomed her own again.

Governor Clinton took up his residence in the De Peyster mansion, on Queen Street (now Pearl), near Cedar, and at once set in motion the government of the new State of New York. In December, aldermen were elected; two months later the governor's council appointed James Duane the first mayor of republican New York, and the city government was complete.

Another and still more dramatic scene occurred in New York during this period, and fitly closes this chapter—the leave-taking of his officers by Washington, the beloved commander in chief. This took place in the "great room" of Fraunces's Tavern, the fashionable hotel of the day, where Washington had fixed his headquarters. Here, on Thursday, December 4, 1783, the general officers assembled for the last farewell. They would never meet again as soldiers of the Continental army.

Washington and many of the bearded warriors are said to have been affected to tears. The former entered the room, and taking a glass of wine in his hand, said: "With a heart filled with love and gratitude, I now take leave of you. I most devoutly wish that your latter days may be as prosperous and happy as your former ones have been glorious and honorable."

Having drained the glass, he continued: "I cannot come to each of you to take my leave, but shall be obliged to you if each will come and take me by the hand."

General Knox, Washington's favorite officer, stood

nearest him, and at these words turned and grasped his hand, and while tears rolled down the cheeks of both the commander in chief kissed him. This he did to all in turn, while sounds of grief filled the room. Soon, however, Washington regained his usual composure, and walked to the Whitehall, followed by a great multitude, who cheered again and again for the savior of his country; but escaping from them, he entered a barge and was rowed to Paulus Hook, where he took stage for Philadelphia and the retirement of Mount Vernon.

## XV. NEW YORK THE CAPITAL CITY.

NEW YORK is the metropolis of America, the second city of the world, yet she may well pride herself on the fact that she was the first capital of the infant republic, that in her borders the Constitution was first tried, the first President inaugurated, and the wheels of national government first set in motion. Washington was elected the first President, as you know. The first Congress under the Constitution was to have met in New York on the 4th of March, 1789, to count the votes for President; but neither the Senate nor the House had a quorum on that day, the members having been delayed by bad roads, swollen rivers, and March mud, so that it was not until the 6th of April that both houses organized and declared George Washington the unanimous choice of the American people for President.

The President elect, apprised at Mount Vernon by official messenger, left his home on the 16th of April, and after a triumphal progress reached New York on the 23d of April. John Adams of Massachusetts, the newly elected Vice President, had preceded him, arriving on the 20th. It took a week to complete the preparations for the inaugural ceremonies, which, as completing the fabric of a national government, it had been decided should be of the most imposing character. On the day appointed, Thursday, April 30, 1789, the thunder of guns aroused the people. At nine o'clock every bell in the city rang a merry peal for a few moments and then suddenly ceased.

The din of traffic was hushed, but the Sabbath silence of the streets was soon broken by the tread of

Washington's Reception at New York.

multitudes in gala attire, citizens and visitors. New York had never before welcomed so many strangers. They came from town and country for a hundred miles around, by packet, stagecoach, and private conveyance, to hail the nativity of a new nation. Each awaited with solemn gladness the commencement of the ceremonies.

After a measured interval the bells began again in

slow, solemn tones, calling the people to the churches to invoke God's blessing on the young nation and its untried President.

After the religious exercises the military escort formed in Cherry Street, opposite the President's home, and as he appeared, attended by a joint committee of the Senate and House of Representatives appointed to escort him to the capitol, formed in columns and took position at the head of the procession. The august body then moved to the capitol in the following order: the sheriff of the city and county of New York, the committee of the Senate, the President elect, the committee of the House, Chancellor Robert R. Livingston, John Jay, Henry Knox, the commissioners of the Treasury, and distinguished citizens in carriages. The capitol was the former City Hall of New York, that stood on the corner of Nassau and Wall streets, where now you see the subtreasury of the United States, with the statue of Washington before it. The building had been remodeled and renovated by Major Pierre L'Enfant, the great French engineer who later laid out the federal city of Washington. The procession marched up Broad Street to Wall, and then halted in front of the capitol; the regiments opened ranks, and Washington and the distinguished company passed through into the capitol, and up the broad stairway to the senate chamber, where both houses of Congress were assembled. As Washington entered, John Adams, the Vice President, and therefore presiding officer of the Senate, arose, advanced, received him with the stately courtesy of the day, and conducted him to the Vice President's chair, which he had just left. Then, after presenting him to the august body, he thus addressed him:

"SIR: The Senate and House of Representatives of the United States are ready to attend you to take the oath required by the Constitution, which will be administered by the chancellor of the State of New York."

"I am ready to proceed," was the President's reply.

Washington and Adams, arm in arm, then walked to a balcony overlooking Wall Street, followed by Chancellor Livingston in his judicial robes, by the senators and representatives. An inspiring sight met their eyes as they emerged upon the gallery. Wall and Broad streets were a sea of upturned faces. All the windows, balconies, and housetops in the vicinity were laden with ladies in gala attire. Flags and banners, caressed by

Inauguration of Washington.

the mild spring zephyrs and bearing the magic name "Washington," waved everywhere. From the whole vast throng not a whisper arose. Soon the confused mass in the balcony resolved itself into three central figures—the noble form of the President on the right, opposite him Chancellor Livingston, and between them the secretary of the Senate, James Otis, holding upon a crimson cushion an open Bible. Then the chancellor, in a voice that reached every ear, repeated the solemn oath:

"You do solemnly swear that you will faithfully execute the office of President of the United States, and will to the best of your ability preserve, protect, and defend the Constitution of the United States."

Washington's Chair at the Inauguration.

"I swear," said Washington, as he bent to kiss the Bible, adding with fervor, "so help me God."

Chancellor Livingston turned to the people, and waving his hand, cried with strong, triumphant voice, "Long live George Washington, President of the United States," and the people answered with resounding cheers, while the spires shook with the pealing of bells, and the air trembled with the thunder of cannon from ship and fort.

For a year New York continued to be the court town. Washington and his cabinet,—Jefferson, Secretary of

State, Hamilton, Secretary of the Treasury, Knox, Secretary of War,—Adams, the Vice President, John Jay, the first chief justice of the United States Supreme Court, Governor George Clinton, and other high officers of government removed their families to the city, and formed a court circle modeled somewhat after that of European capitals.

There was far more of stately ceremonial and etiquette about official life in those days than now. For instance, the President delivered his messages to Congress in person, after the fashion of the English kings, instead of sending them by his secretary as now. In his diary for January 8, 1790, Washington gives an interesting account of this ceremony. He set out at eleven o'clock for Federal Hall, he tells us, in a coach drawn by six horses, preceded by his secretary, Colonel Humphreys, and Major Johnson on horseback, followed by Messrs. Lear and Nelson in his chariot, and by Mr. Lewis on horseback. In their rear came the chief justice of the United States and the secretaries of the Treasury and War departments in their carriages. As he entered all rose, and remained standing until he sat. After all were seated he rose and delivered his speech, and then gave one copy to the president of the Senate and another to the Speaker of the House, after which he bowed and retired with his party.

In a few days Congress returned an answer to the speech, "the members of both [houses] coming in carriages" for the purpose, and "the answer of the Senate being presented by the Vice President, and that of the House by the Speaker,"

A Ball in Washington's Time.

In the social amenities of the day Washington figured prominently. He leased a house, at first Mr. Osgood's, and later the McComb mansion on Broadway, a little south of Trinity Church, and removed thither with his wife, his horses, carriages, and retinue of servants, from Mount Vernon. He entertained generously, and was entertained with equal hospitality. At one time, we read, he honored Secretary and Mrs. Hamilton and several others with tickets to his private box in the John Street theater. At another, after a dinner party he went with Mrs. Washington to the dancing assembly and remained there until ten o'clock. On Christmas day he "went to St. Paul's Chapel in the forenoon." The houses of Jay, Hamilton, Vice President Adams, and Governor Clinton were also centers of social courtesies during this period.

Meantime the question of a permanent site for a capital was agitating the nation. New York would doubtless have been chosen, but the State was not willing to cede the ten miles square of territory demanded. Philadelphia's claims were warmly advocated, but Southern congressmen objected, because her Quakers were "eternally dogging Southern members with their schemes of emancipation." Virginia, Maryland, and other Southern States advocated a site on the Potomac, which after much discussion was adopted; but while our present capital city of Washington was being built Congress decided to hold its sessions in Philadelphia, and when it rose on the 12th of August, 1790, it adjourned to meet in that city the next December.

## XVI. THE GROWTH OF PARTIES.

FOR the first few years after the war the law offered the best field to the strong and ardent spirits of the day. Litigation was rife,—confiscated estates, civil boundaries, debts of individuals and States, gave large employment to the courts,—while the law then, as now, was the door to political preferment. There were two parties from the beginning, Federalist and Republican, first defined by the struggle over the Constitution, but still very loosely organized. The Federalist was styled by its opponents the "English party." Its leaders regarded the British Constitution as the most perfect that could be devised, and wished to pattern the American Constitution after it. They disliked and distrusted France, and advocated a strong central government, a standing army, a diplomatic service like that of European nations, a restriction of the suffrage, and encouragement of domestic industries by a protective tariff.

The Republicans, on the other hand, stood for State rights and powers; they advocated the utmost simplicity and economy in government, the doing away with the state and etiquette of courts, a well-drilled militia instead of a standing army, open sessions of Congress, an extension of the franchise, free trade, and the encouragement of agriculture and internal trade rather than of foreign commerce. Washington, Adams, and Hamilton were the recognized leaders of the Federalists; Jefferson, Madison, and, later, Aaron Burr, of the Republicans.

The successful working of the new Constitution, which was based largely on Federal principles, placed the Federalists in power, and this advantage they maintained for the first eleven years of our national life. But in the presidential election of 1800 a condition arose in our city of New York which defeated them.

There were two able men then living in New York, rivals in law, politics, and other things, Alexander Hamilton and Aaron Burr. Hamilton was the superior of Burr in statesmanship and depth of intellect, but was far excelled by the latter in tact, executive force, and mastery over men. Burr had been senator from New York 1791-1796, and in the presidential election of 1796 had received thirty electoral votes for President. In 1796 he had been defeated for reëlection to the Senate by the Federalists under Hamilton's leadership, and in revenge set to work to wrest New York from them in the approaching presidential contest of 1800, seeing clearly that with the vote of New York the Republicans could elect their candidate for President. Presidential electors at that time were chosen by the State legislatures; Burr therefore caused himself to be elected to the legislature of New York, and, while there, with favors and compliments made himself popular with rural members, whom he knew to possess great influence over their constituents at home. He was also in constant communication with his party leaders in other States, and arranged with them a plan of campaign.

As the year 1800 approached, he bent all his marvelous powers so to organize and discipline the Republican party in New York as to win victory at the polls. He began by gathering about him a body of able, ardent, resolute spirits, young lawyers mostly, ambitious to rise, and imparted to them his courage and energy. They were the "ward workers,"—a term now for the first time known in American politics,—who attended primaries and caucuses, and got out the full vote, nay, more, made lists of the whole body of freemen, noting the name, age, habits, residence, health, and religion of each, for the use of their principal.

You must remember that at this time New York was Federal in politics. John Jay was governor. In the State election of 1799 the Republicans had been beaten by a majority of nine hundred votes. In April, 1800, the legislature which would elect presidential electors was to be chosen. Burr bent every effort to make it Republican: he nominated only the strongest men— George Clinton, so long governor of New York, General Horatio Gates, the conqueror of Burgoyne, Samuel Osgood, Washington's Postmaster General, and others of equal standing; he held ward and general meetings and addressed them in his nervous, vigorous, fiery way, supervised his ward workers, and noted every move of his adversary with the eye of a lynx.

Alexander Hamilton.

Hamilton, who again led the Federalists, also threw

all his heart and soul into this contest. It was the bitterest political conflict the young nation had yet seen. As election day approached the result was felt to be doubtful. The polls opened on the 29th of April, and continued open for three days. It was a time of great excitement in the city. Newspapers, broadsides, pamphlets, flew about like leaves in autumn. From large platforms the rival leaders addressed the people, often by turns, one listening while the other spoke, and then rising and replying.

At sunset on May 2 the polls closed, and before the electors slept they knew that the Republicans had carried the city by four hundred and ninety votes, which made the State Republican, and insured the success of the Republican candidates for President and Vice President, Thomas Jefferson and Aaron Burr.

Out of the strife and bitterness engendered in this conflict grew the duel between General Hamilton and Colonel Burr on July 11, 1804, which consigned Hamilton to the grave, and made Burr an outcast and wanderer on the earth.

After the presidential contest of 1804 officious friends bore to Colonel Burr certain remarks reflecting on his character said to have been uttered by General Hamilton. By and by these remarks were printed in one of the party organs in the city. Colonel Burr at once sent the newspaper by a friend to General Hamilton, and demanded an acknowledgment or denial of the use of such expressions. General Hamilton replied that if Colonel Burr would single out any one expression or statement he would deny or acknowledge it, but he could not undertake to give a general denial or acknowledgment as to what he had or had not said in the heat of political debate for a period of several years.

Colonel Burr replied that the remarks said to have been made by General Hamilton cast dishonor upon him, and again demanded that General Hamilton should deny them or take the consequences. General Hamilton refusing to deny, a challenge was given and accepted.

The duel, savage and murderous as we now justly regard it, was then the recognized mode among gentlemen of settling affairs of this sort. Both Burr and Hamilton had recognized it. A few years before, Hamilton's eldest son, a youth of great promise, had fallen in a duel. Burr had been a principal in one of the savage affairs. The partisans of both had fought for the honor of their chiefs and with their approval. For either of the latter to have refused to fight at this juncture would have been to sacrifice his posi-

The Duel between Burr and Hamilton.

tion in society and fall in public esteem. And so, although Hamilton at heart detested the code, they met on the " dark and bloody ground " of Weehawken, sacred to these encounters.

The station of the West Shore Railroad is a little north of the bench in the cliff where the duel took place, but on the verge of the crag above you will find

Hamilton's Residence.

a small stone pillar with an inscription which nearly marks its location.

Hamilton fell at the first fire, mortally wounded. Burr escaped unharmed. The fainting statesman was rowed across the river and tenderly carried to the residence nearest at hand, that of Mr. Bayard of Greenwich, his own beautiful country seat, " the Grange," in the northern part of the island, being too far away to be reached by one in his condition. Servants were hastily sent for surgeons and nurses, and Mrs. Hamilton and the children summoned.

The fatal meeting occurred at sunrise. The victim died at two o'clock next day. The news rapidly spread through the city, and called from all classes expressions of grief, pity, and sympathy, mingled with execrations on the slayer.

At a meeting of the merchants held the same evening it was resolved to close the stores on the day of the funeral, to wear crape for thirty days, and to order the flags on the shipping at half-mast.

The lawyers met next morning and agreed to wear mourning for six weeks. The Society of the Cincinnati, the Tammany Society, the students of Columbia College, the St. Andrew's Society, the General Society of Mechanics, the various military companies, the corporation of the city, all passed resolutions of sympathy, and pledged themselves to attend the funeral in a body.

The statesman's death occurred on Thursday afternoon. His funeral was held in Trinity Church the succeeding Saturday. A more imposing pageant than the funeral cortége as it moved slowly down Broadway, amid the booming of minute guns from the Battery and war ships in the bay, the city had never seen. When all were assembled in the church, with the four sons of the dead statesman beside him, the eldest sixteen, the youngest four, Gouverneur Morris, the lifelong friend of Hamilton, delivered an eloquent and pathetic funeral oration.

Thus tragically passed from the scene one of the

greatest spirits New York has ever numbered among her citizens—

> THE PATRIOT OF INCORRUPTIBLE INTEGRITY,
> THE SOLDIER OF APPROVED VALOR,
> THE STATESMAN OF CONSUMMATE WISDOM,

as one may read on his modest tombstone in Trinity churchyard.

His honest fame is the city's heritage. For our instruction let us glance at the salient points of his career. Born in the West Indian island of St. Nevis in 1757, his father a Scotch merchant, his mother a French lady of good family, he was sent in boyhood to a grammar school at Elizabethtown, New Jersey, and as soon as he was fitted entered King's College in New York. His first public appearance was when the disagreement between Great Britain and her colonies began. Although but eighteen, he wrote a series of papers in defense of the rights of the colonists, which were so able that they were at first thought to have been written by the eminent statesman John Jay, and they gained him the notice and respect of the patriot leaders. During the Revolution he was at first in command of a company of artillery, and later the aid-de-camp and trusted friend and admirer of Washington. In 1782 he was admitted to the bar, and the same year was elected a representative from New York to the Continental Congress, in 1786 a member of the New York legislature, and in 1787 a delegate to the convention which met at Philadelphia, as it was said, to revise the old Articles of Confederation, but which really produced the Constitution under which we have since lived.

Hamilton and Madison were the chief authors of that instrument. After being adopted by the convention it had to be ratified by the States before it could become the law of the land. Several States were opposed to it, New York among them, and to overcome their objections and silence cavilers, Hamilton, Jay, and Madison wrote a series of masterly state papers, which first appeared in the New York "Daily Advertiser," and were later collected and published as "The Federalist." Of the eighty-five papers in that work fifty-one were written by Hamilton.

When the new government went into effect in 1789, Washington appointed Hamilton Secretary of the Treasury, and in this capacity he originated the fiscal policy of the young nation, and rescued it from the condition of bankruptcy and ruined credit in which the war had left it. In 1795 he resigned this office to resume the practice of the law in New York, and so continued until his death.

In New York the popular feeling against his slayer was for a time intense. Although holding the exalted office of Vice President of the United States, Burr was indicted for murder, and would probably have been arrested had he remained in the city. Later, as you know, he was arrested on a charge of treason, tried at Richmond in Virginia, and acquitted, but fearing a second arrest, fled to Europe. Good came of his act, however, for it brought dueling into disrepute, and abolished from polite society that savage and barbarous outgrowth of feudalism.

The heated contest of 1800 taught politicians the power of party discipline, and led to the birth of the present Tammany Society as a political organization. This now powerful society had been founded in 1789 by moderate men of both parties as a patriotic and benevolent order, with a view also of counteracting the influence of the Society of the Cincinnati, which had been founded by the surviving officers of the Revolution soon after the war, and which many thought aristocratic and unrepublican. The Tammany Society was intended also to placate the Indians and protect them in their rights. To this end it was named after a famous Indian chief, Tammany, and adopted Indian names, forms, and ceremonies, the year being divided into seasons,—blossoms, fruits, and snows,—and the seasons into moons. The members were called "braves;" the officers comprised thirteen "sachems" (who elected a "grand sachem"), a sagamore, and a winkinskie. John Pintard was the first sagamore; the grand sachem in 1791 was Josiah Ogden Hoffman, and the scribe of the council De Witt Clinton. In the spring of 1791 John Pintard, the real founder of the society, wrote to a friend in Boston: "This being a strong national society, I ingrafted an antiquarian scheme of a museum upon it. It makes small progress with a small fund and may succeed. We have a tolerable collection of pamphlets, mostly modern, with some history, of which I will send you an abstract."

This "museum" became in 1804 the present New York Historical Society, and its collection was the nucleus of the priceless treasures of books, pamphlets, newspapers, paintings, relics, and curios now owned by that society, but hidden and of little avail because of the want of a suitable building in which to display them.

After the contests of 1800 and 1804, as before remarked, Tammany became more and more a political organization, and has since almost continuously held political control of the city of New York, chiefly because of the stern discipline and admirable political machinery first set in motion by Aaron Burr in 1800.

## XVII. HER RISE TO COMMERCIAL POWER.

THE genius of New York is commercial and financial; her proud position as metropolis of the western continent is due alike to her merchants, manufacturers, and financiers, and to her situation on an island, with a great navigable river on one side, an arm of the sea on the other, and an unrivaled harbor before. These alone would have made her a queen of traffic even if the genius of man had not created the canal and railroad to bring to her warehouses the products of the mines, fields, and forests of nearly four million square miles of territory.

Almost immediately on gaining her freedom the young city began extending her commerce. Trade with England and her colonies revived. The starry flag became a familiar object in French, German, and Russian ports. In a few years New York had won her share of the rich trade of the Mediterranean, and a little later competed with the merchants of Salem and Boston for the priceless fabrics, the gems, teas, and spices of China and India. It was not until after the War of 1812-1815, however, that she began that marvelous growth and development which in less than a century has made her the second city of the world. In 1783 she had 23,000 inhabitants; in 1810, 95,000; in 1898, 3,389,753. This growth, in addition to the natural causes before cited, has been brought about by three beneficent genii that about 1815 came to her aid—the steamboat, the canal, and the railroad.

The steamboat came first, Fulton's historic *Clermont* having been the first to make a successful voyage. She steamed up the Hudson to Albany in 1807, frightening half out of their wits the simple countrymen and river men, who thought her some grisly visitor from the nether world.

Clermont.

Her inventor, Robert Fulton, was one of the greatest men of his age. Like many other great men, he was of humble lineage, having been born on a farm in Little Britain (now Fulton), near Lancaster, Pennsylvania, in the year 1765. He was a talented painter, but is chiefly remembered for his inventions and discoveries in mechanical science—steamboats, torpedo boats, and improvements in canals and canal boats. Ferryboats, and the movable slips into which they run, were among his most notable inventions.

After many experiments, trials, and failures the *Clermont* was at length finished. Then it was advertised that she would sail for Albany on her trial trip on the morning of August 11, 1807. A great crowd gathered at the dock to see her depart, for many witticisms had been launched at her and her projector while she was building, and few believed that she could be forced against wind and tide by the power of vapor "confined in a kettle." But the *Clermont* steamed steadily northward on her way to Albany, and those who had come to laugh went away to wonder, gossip, and admire.

Robert Fulton.

Her maiden voyage proved a complete success. She arrived at "Clermont," Mr. Livingston's country seat, a distance of one hundred and ten miles, in twenty-four hours, and at Albany in eight hours more, making the entire distance of one hundred and fifty miles in thirty-two hours, against both wind and tide. Of course this was a very slow passage compared with that of our modern palatial steamers which make the distance in a night, but when set over against the time of the packet sloops—from four to seven days—it was deemed a marvelous achievement.

Fulton had two powerful friends in Joel Barlow, the poet and statesman, and Robert R. Livingston, the former of whom advanced him money to begin his experiments in Paris, while the latter became his partner in building the *Clermont*, and secured for her owners the exclusive privilege of navigating the waters of New York for a term of years.

The *Clermont* at once began making regular trips to Albany as a passenger boat, never lacking for patronage. Soon rival boats were built and placed on the river in defiance of the exclusive privilege given to Fulton and Livingston, who had recourse to the courts to protect their rights. By 1809 there was a regular weekly line of steam packets to Albany. By 1813 this had grown to a triweekly line, the boats leaving New York every Tuesday, Thursday, and Saturday afternoon.

Meanwhile inventors were busily engaged improving on the original boat, and by 1817 the time of passage had been reduced to eighteen hours. In 1818 the present steamboat service on Long Island Sound was begun, the *Fulton*, under Fulton and Livingston's patent, plying between New York and New Haven, and the *Connecticut*, an independent boat, making regular trips to New London. In 1822 the New York and Providence line, the nucleus of the present Sound lines to Boston, was formed. By 1830 there were eighty-six steamboats running on New York waters.

A year before this, a man had settled in New York who was destined to become a great factor in the commercial development of the city—Cornelius Vanderbilt. He had been born at Port Richmond on Staten Island thirty-five years before, a poor boy, but strong in body and mind, and intent on rising in the world. At sixteen he had saved money enough to buy a sailboat, and with it opened a ferry between Staten Island and New York. The venture proved profitable, and at eighteen he owned two boats and had saved one thousand dollars in money.

Cornelius Vanderbilt.

The steamboat early attracted his attention. The traffic would not warrant placing one on his Staten Island route, and Fulton and Livingston had a monopoly of the Hudson and the Sound; but he saw that a line might be operated to New Brunswick, New Jersey, there connecting with stages to Philadelphia, and in 1817, at the age of twenty-three, with nine thousand dollars in the bank, he joined another steamboat financier, Thomas Gibbons, in building a small steamer to run to New Brunswick. When he left this line in 1829 it was paying forty thousand dollars a year. But in 1829 Fulton and Livingston's monopoly of the Hudson and Sound ceased, and Vanderbilt saw opening before him a wider field.

He removed to New York, and entered with ardor on the business of transportation in New York waters, soon making his presence felt. He found the steamboat service of the day wretched, the boats small and slow, the cabins filthy and ill ventilated, the rates of fare high. At once he set about building large, new, full-powered boats, and at the same time reduced fares, the result being that in a short time he was practically in control of the Sound and river traffic.

His success naturally raised up competitors,—Colonel John Stevens, Dean Richmond, Daniel Drew, kings of finance and transportation,—but Commodore Vanderbilt distanced them all. Between 1829 and 1848 he owned and operated nearly fifty steamboats, most of which were built for him. The California gold excitement of 1849 led him into ocean steamship ventures, and he founded an opposition line to that of the Pacific Mail Steamship Company, the prize being the passenger traffic to California across the Isthmus of Darien. This resulted in his opponents buying him off, as there was not trade enough for both.

Daniel Drew.

Dean Richmond.

A little later, in 1855, he established a line of steamers from New York to Havre, France, which, being larger, swifter, and better appointed than the Collins line, then running to England, soon gained large patronage. This line he continued until the breaking out of the Civil War, in 1860, swept American commerce from the ocean. After that event Mr. Vanderbilt turned his attention to the railroad, the great rival of the steamboat and canal.

## XVIII. THE ERIE CANAL.

THE second chief factor, in point of time, in the building up of New York was the canal. Fulton had suggested it as early as 1786, railroads being then unthought of. Washington, George Clinton, and Elkanah Watson early advocated a canal from Albany to the Great Lakes. After the steamboat was invented, the fact that boats could be towed by steam from New York to Albany, and the slight elevation of the divide between the head waters of the Mohawk River and the basin of the Great Lakes, no doubt first suggested the idea of a canal from Albany to Buffalo, which should connect the Lakes with the Atlantic, and give to New York the commerce of half a continent. After some private agitation the project was brought to the attention of the New York legislature in 1810–1811, but was dismissed by that body as being beyond the resources of New York, even if the "big ditch," as its opponents termed it in derision, could be dug. In 1815, however, after the war, with the revival of trade and the marvelous development of the West, the project was revived, this time by the merchants of New York, with De Witt Clinton, then mayor, afterwards governor, at their head. A meeting was held at the City Hall in the autumn of 1815, at which a committee was appointed, with Mayor

Clinton as chairman, to prepare a memorial to the incoming legislature on the subject. That memorial, written by Clinton, was one of the ablest and most far-reaching in its effects of any state paper of the period. It pictured in glowing terms the benefits to State and city of the gigantic undertaking It would make tributary to them the Great Lakes and the empire of the Northwest yet to be. Boats laden with the products of that vast region would pass through it in endless procession. Agriculture would build her granaries, and commerce her storehouses, along its banks. Great manufactories would spring up. Towns and cities would mark its course.

De Witt Clinton.

In addition to these predictions, which time has fulfilled in every particular, the paper told the legislators how to build the canal, what the cost would be, and how money could be raised to meet it.

A bill chartering it was introduced in the legislature of 1817, and at once engaged the attention of the whole State. The newspapers were filled with arguments *pro* and *con*. Monster mass meetings in its favor were held in New York and along the line of the proposed canal.

In the legislature there was much opposition, but after a stormy debate the bill was passed on April 17, 1817.

On July 4, 1817, ground was first broken for the canal at Rome, midway between the two termini. The work was so stupendous that it appealed to the imagination of all classes. Most of the right of way was given. The wealthy subscribed to the stock; the sturdy yeomen along the line worked with willing hands, looking forward to the bridal of the sea and lakes, and to the added power and glory of the State.

By 1820 the middle section, from Utica to Rome, ninety-six miles, had been opened. On October 1, 1823, the eastern section, from Utica to Albany, was completed, and in 1825 the whole canal was declared ready for traffic. The herculean work, that its opponents said would require the labor of a generation and tax the financial resources of a nation, had been completed in a little more than eight years.

The people determined that its completion should be celebrated in a fitting and proper manner. Perhaps there was more poetry and sentiment in men's minds then than in this utilitarian age, for this celebration was certainly one of the most original and dramatic in the history of peoples.

At precisely ten o'clock on the morning of the 26th of October, 1825, the waters of Lake Erie rushed into the canal, and the fleet of canal boats began its journey. At the same instant the first signal gun at Buffalo was fired. Its report, repeated by relays of cannon, swept over the broad reaches of the lake basin to Rochester, across the Genesee's flats to Syracuse, over the sixty-seven-mile level to Utica, and down the beautiful valley of the Mohawk to Albany. At 11 A.M. to a moment, the grim old veteran standing to his piece at Castleton caught the signal gun from Albany, and applied his match. Coxsackie caught it at 11:03, Hudson one minute later, Catskill, Upper Red Hook, Rhinebeck, and Hyde Park at moment intervals. At 11:09 it reached Poughkeepsie, and the eagles on Storm King screamed with joy, thinking war had come again. Hamburg, Newburg, West Point, Fort Montgomery, Stony Point, Sing Sing, Closters Landing, Fort Washington, Fort Gansevoort, the Battery, Fort Lafayette, received it in succession and sent it thundering on, the last station—Sandy Hook—receiving it at 11:21 A.M., twenty-one minutes after it left Albany, and one hour and twenty-one minutes from Buffalo. This did not equal the speed of the telegraph, but it was certainly

Model of a Canal Packet Boat.

more impressive and romantic. At twenty-two minutes past eleven o'clock Fort Lafayette began the return fire, which reached Buffalo at ten minutes before one, the sound having traveled over eleven hundred miles in less than three hours.

Let us return to the four pioneer boats which at the moment of the inrushing of the waters began their journey eastward. First came the *Seneca Chief*, drawn by four spirited gray horses in elegant harness, and following her, the *Superior*, the *Commodore Perry*, a freight boat, and the *Buffalo* of Erie. They bore as invited guests a distinguished company—De Witt Clinton, then governor of New York, Lieutenant Governor Tallmadge, the delegation from New York appointed to extend the hospitalities of the city to the distinguished company, and a large number of fair women and eminent men.

As the fleet moved slowly along, the people of the entire State seemed to have massed themselves on the banks to greet it.

At Rochester the canal had been carried over the Genesee River by a massive stone aqueduct of nine arches, each of fifty feet span. At the entrance to this a sentinel boat had been stationed, and as the fleet approached hailed it.

"Who comes there?"

"Your brothers from the West, on the waters of the Great Lakes," was the reply.

"By what means have they been diverted so far from their natural course?" was the next query.

"Through the channel of the grand Erie Canal."

"By whose authority and by whom was a work of such magnitude accomplished?" asked the voice.

"By the authority and by the enterprise of the people of the State of New York," came the reply.

The sentinel boat then gave way, and allowed the fleet to glide over the aqueduct and enter the spacious basin at its eastern end amid the cheers of thousands and welcoming salutes of artillery. Similar demonstrations awaited them all along the line.

On the morning of November 4 the fleet was abreast of the Palisades, with the great city gleaming dimly in the mellow autumn haze. An hour later it anchored off the city, and soon after was boarded by a committee of the common council, which, through its spokesman, Alderman Cowdrey, welcomed the party to the city. Several hours later a great naval procession was formed, and proceeded to the Brooklyn Navy Yard, whence, after taking on board officers and guests, it steamed out to sea.

The scene at this moment must have been an animated one. There were twenty-nine steam vessels of all sorts in line, while the bay was covered with ships, frigates, steamers, barges, and other craft, each bedecked with bunting from trucks to keelson, and swarming with humanity, while both shores, the heights on the north and east, and the islands of the harbor were covered with applauding spectators. In advance was the official steamer *Washington*, with the mayor, corporation, and distinguished guests on board. As the flotilla neared the Narrows it was met by a graceful pilot boat, which hailed and announced that it had been sent by Neptune to conduct the fleet to his capital.

That capital at this moment was the United States schooner *Porpoise*, anchored just within Sandy Hook, and the fleet proceeded to surround it, forming a circle some three miles in circumference. Then Neptune hailed them from his throne and put the usual questions as to whence they came, and their business there. When he had been satisfied, the last act in the pretty drama was performed. Governor Clinton, handsome in face, manly in form, gallant of spirit, standing

The Ceremony in the Bay.

in the bow of the *Seneca Chief*, took a keg of water which had been brought from Lake Erie, and holding it aloft in full view of all, poured its contents into the sea, saying:

"This solemnity, at this place, on the first arrival of vessels from Lake Erie, is intended to indicate and commemorate the navigable communication which has been accomplished between our mediterranean seas and the Atlantic Ocean, in about eight years, to the extent of more than four hundred and twenty-five miles, by the wisdom, public spirit, and energy of the people of the State of New York; and may the God of the heavens and the earth smile most propitiously on this work, and render it subservient to the best interests of the human race."

Dr. Mitchill then poured into the ocean water from the Nile, Indus, Ganges, Thames, and other rivers, and the ceremony was complete.

After the return of the company to the Battery there was a great land procession, and the corporation further marked the day by issuing a large number of medals in gold, silver, and white metal.

Thus the stupendous work was completed, and began its mission of building up a commercial metropolis; for the Erie Canal has been one of the greatest factors in the city's marvelous growth, diverting to her most of the crude products of the great West, and distributing there the myriad commodities imported by her merchants from foreign shores.

## XIX. THE RAILROAD.

SIX years later, in 1831, a competitor appeared which in the course of a generation was destined wholly to supersede the canal as a means of passenger transportation, and to a large extent in the moving of freight, although the lower freight tariff by water still makes the influence of the canal felt. In 1831 the first railroad in New York, and one of the first in the United States, was opened between Albany and Schenectady.

A year later, April 24, 1832, was chartered the first great trunk line, the Erie, designed to open communication between the city of New York and the Great Lakes through the southern counties of the State. It was not until 1851, however, that this colossal enterprise was completed, and New York connected by railroad with the prairies of the West.

During the same period the Mohawk and Hudson Railroad had been pushing westward from Albany, under various names, up the Mohawk valley, side by side with the canal, until in 1854, by the completion of the Buffalo and Lockport Railroad, it formed a continuous line of rail from Albany to Buffalo. These various roads had been consolidated into one in 1853, under the name of the New York Central Railroad. The latter was consolidated with the Hudson River Railroad, from New York to Albany, in 1869, under the title of the New York Central and Hudson River Railroad, the two roads forming the second great trunk line between New York and the West. Two years later the Pennsylvania Railroad, which had been opened from Philadelphia to Pittsburg in 1854, secured control of the united railways of New Jersey, and formed the third great trunk line. There have since been added the Baltimore and Ohio, the Delaware, Lackawanna and Western, the Lehigh Valley, and the West Shore, making in all seven trunk lines connecting New York with the West and South. These seven great highways, with her waterways, her geographical position, and her unexcelled harbor, must assure to New York future commercial supremacy, provided her merchants have the foresight and energy to take advantage of them.

## XX. TYPICAL NEW YORK MERCHANTS.

IN the winter of 1784 there arrived in Baltimore a fair-haired German youth of twenty-one, with a small stock of goods which he had bought in London. He had no other capital except thrift, energy, good habits, and an invincible determination to succeed. His name was John Jacob Astor. He had met on shipboard a fellow-countryman, by trade a furrier, who told him of the business opportunities of the fur trade even for men of small capital, and the young adventurer determined to become a fur merchant.

John Jacob Astor.

He accordingly came on to New York, sold his goods, and with the proceeds purchased furs, which were bought of the Indians and trappers, who still came to New York to sell the products of their winter's toil. With these he went to London, sold them at a large profit, and returned to New York with the purpose of learning all that could be learned about the fur business.

First he apprenticed himself to a furrier and mastered the mechanical part of the trade. A few years later he opened a store of his own. But he was not long content with a retail tradesman's position. His inquiring and comprehensive mind reached out after the fur trade of North America, which at this time was nearly as valuable to the English as the gold and silver of South American mines had been to the Spanish.

He found that the central mart of furs in North America was Montreal, Canada. All the trade in furs of that vast region stretching from the Great Lakes to the head waters of the Mississippi and Missouri, later called the Northwest, had been first carried on by the French traders of Canada, when that country belonged to France. After the British conquest the trade of course fell to Englishmen.

This territory, he found, was now (1790) covered by three great rival companies: the Hudson Bay Company, chartered in 1670 by Charles II., and given exclusive right to trap and trade in the region watered by Hudson Bay and its tributaries; the Northwest Company, founded in 1787, which controlled by its fortified trading posts the whole region of the upper lakes; and the Mackinaw Company, younger in years, whose headquarters were on Mackinac Island, at the mouth of Lake Michigan, and whose posts cordoned the latter lake and stretched along the Fox and Wisconsin rivers and across to the very head waters of the Mississippi. The fur-bearing animals, such as the beaver, mink, otter, fox, wolf, and muskrat, were then trapped by the Indians and half-breeds, and their pelts conveyed to the company's forts to be exchanged for powder, ball, firearms, blankets, trinkets, calicoes, and other goods attractive to the Indian.

Then, once a year, with the high water of spring, great fleets of canoes and boats, filled with goods, would set out from Montreal, ascend the Ottawa River, and thence by other rivers and portages reach Lakes Huron and Superior and the most distant posts, exchange their goods for furs, and return with the latter to Montreal.

Having possessed himself of these details, our merchant determined as soon as he could to enter into this country himself; but for the present he was content to buy his furs in Montreal and ship them thence direct to London, Canada being at that time forbidden to trade with any but the mother country. In 1795, however, England made a treaty with us which allowed our merchants to trade direct with Canada, and from that time Mr. Astor's furs were sent direct to New York. Some of them were reshipped to Europe, some sold at home, but the most of them were sent to China, our merchant being a pioneer in the China trade, which later became so extensive and profitable. The Chinese prized furs highly and were willing to pay handsomely for them. Mr. Astor would therefore ship his cargoes of fur to Canton, and bring back in return tea, silks, chinaware, fireworks, nankeens, and other commodities. These ventures proved immensely profitable, and he was soon in a position to set in motion his scheme of an American fur company in the Northwest.

The Mackinaw Company, under British control, conducted its operations almost wholly in United States territory. Mr. Astor now decided to occupy this field, and instead of bringing his furs half across a continent and then shipping them around Cape Horn to China, to ship them direct from a port on the Pacific Ocean. Our government, then under the statesmanlike Jefferson, heartily approved of this plan, as it had long viewed with alarm the influence possessed by alien trappers and traders over the Indian tribes in our territory.

In 1809 the State of New York chartered the American Fur Company, with a capital of one million dollars, with power to increase it to two million. This company was really John Jacob Astor, he owning all of its stock and controlling its movements; but he wished the authority of a State charter in order to cope with the Mackinaw Company, a wealthy and powerful corporation. He at once entered the field against the latter company, but the rivalry proved so intense, and the collisions between the partisans of the two companies so frequent, that in 1811 he bought out the rival company. He would now, no doubt, have been very successful had not the war of 1812 with England broken out and stopped further operations by calling the hunters and trappers on both sides to arms.

He had previously conceived a grander scheme, that of carrying out his project of a fur company on the Pacific coast. In 1810, you must remember, the vast region now occupied by the great States of Oregon, Washington, Idaho, and Wyoming was an unknown wilderness. The famous navigator Captain Cook, during his last voyage, 1776–1779, had skirted the Pacific shore and reported the presence there of sea otter in large numbers. Now, the fur of this animal was highly prized in China, and by 1791 there were a score of vessels, chiefly from Boston and Salem, on this coast collecting sea otter fur. One of these vessels, the *Columbia*, Captain Gray, of Boston, had discovered the great estuary of the Columbia, and had sailed up that river for some distance, Captain Gray calling it after his vessel, the *Columbia;* but none had ever ascended to its fountain-head amid the eternal snows of the Rocky Mountains, a thousand miles inland. This region was virgin soil. No organized company had ever obtained a foothold there, for the posts of the Russian Fur Company were far to the northward. Mr. Astor now proposed to establish a colony of trappers and traders at the mouth of the Columbia, with posts stretching back to its sources and up and down the coast, the whole to be supplied by his vessels, which would receive in return the furs gathered by the trappers, convey them to China, and there load with return cargoes for New York.

This plan he proceeded to execute with his accustomed energy. With Mr. Wilson Hunt of New Jersey and others he formed the Pacific Fur Company, and dispatched a large ship, the *Tonquin*, around the Horn with everything necessary for a colony and for the Indian trade. Three of his partners sailed in the ship, with a number of colonists. They built a village at the mouth of the Columbia, which they called Astoria, after the founder, and the enterprise seemed destined to succeed.

But it was the victim of a series of misfortunes, which

in the end led its founder to relinquish it. First, the *Tonquin* was captured by the Indians while on a trading voyage to the northward, and all of her crew except five, who managed to escape, were massacred. To avenge their loss, Mr. Lewis, the supercargo, who had been seriously wounded and left on the ship, blew her up while the Indians were dancing and feasting on board.

Mr. Hunt, who had left Montreal in August, 1810, with a large party, to come overland, reached his destination only after enduring incredible hardships and suffering the loss of everything but life itself. A second ship, sent out in 1811, found the little colony at Astoria in good health and spirits, and the trading posts which had been established well equipped and prosperous. But the outbreak of the war soon after led Mr. Astor to sell his whole interest on the Pacific coast to the Northwest Company for about half its value. You will find the whole romantic and interesting story of this enterprise graphically told in Washington Irving's "Astoria."

Mr. Astor's later ventures were not of such national importance, although they reached to the remotest seas. He retired from commercial life about twenty years before his death, and devoted himself to the care of his real estate interests, which had grown to large proportions. His tastes were scholarly, and at his modest mansion, which stood on the site of the present Astor House, he delighted to gather about him the scholars and literary men of his day. One of these was Washington Irving, a handsome, graceful youth, a lawyer without briefs, who in 1809 awoke one morning to find himself famous as the author of the "History of New York, by Diedrich Knickerbocker." Another of these guests was Fitz-Greene Halleck, the poet whose "Marco Bozzaris" you have so often declaimed, and who was employed in Mr. Astor's counting-house. On his death in 1848 Mr. Astor still further showed his regard for letters by leaving three hundred and fifty thousand dollars for the endowment of the Astor Library.

We have given his story somewhat in detail as showing what enterprises of moment were undertaken by New York merchants in those days.

Another striking venture of this period was that of the good ship *Betsey*, which in 1797 was sent on a voyage round the world by a company of New York merchants, with a view of discovering commercial openings in the South Seas and Pacific Ocean. The *Betsey* had been gone two years when, in 1799, she suddenly appeared in the Narrows, and sailed up to her berth at the Fly Market wharf, filled to her hatches with tea, silk, chinaware, cassia, and nankeens, and with her crew of healthy young sailors paraded on deck, clad in jackets of China silk, yellow nankeen trousers, and bleached chip hats trimmed with blue ribbons. Every man before the mast received one thousand dollars and costly silks for his share of the venture, while the profits of the principals were fabulous. This voyage led to the rich trade of New York with the Orient.

There were many other great merchants of a later period. Howland & Aspinwall were prominent from

1831 to 1840. They were the pioneers in the Pacific trade, and did the largest general business of any firm, with the Mediterranean, England, the East and West Indies. They owned a fleet of seventeen or eighteen ships, among them several Liverpool packets. A single cargo of theirs sent to the Pacific coast of South America

Broadway, 1840.

was often worth two hundred and fifty thousand dollars, and comprised pretty much everything from a cambric needle to a hoop pole, the minor articles being packed in small barrels to go on mules' backs over the Andes. For this firm was built one of the first of the famous clipper ships to sail out of New York, as will be more fully narrated in a subsequent chapter.

N. L. & G. Griswold were the greatest China merchants of this period. Their ship would sail from New York in May with a cargo of ginseng, spelter, lead, iron, etc., worth thirty thousand dollars, and one hundred and seventy thousand Spanish dollars in specie, reach Whampoa, the port of Canton, in due time, be loaded by her supercargo in two months with tea, chinaware, and cassia, or false cinnamon, but principally with tea, and return to New York within the year. The tea cost thirty-seven cents a pound in China, and paid a duty in

New York of seventy-five cents a pound. The first cost of a cargo was about $200,000; the duties and expenses raised it to $600,000. The cargo would be sold to the wholesale dealer for $700,000, the merchants taking his notes for four and six months. But the duties were not payable until nine, twelve, and sometimes eighteen months after entry, so that the importer had the use of nearly $400,000 for that period, in addition to his profit of $100,000 on a cargo.

This was the usual course pursued by the other great China merchants, Astor, Grinnell, Minturn & Co., A. A. Low & Brother, Thomas H. Smith & Sons, and others. By and by Smith & Sons failed, owing the government about three million dollars in unpaid duties. The loss of this amount led to a change in the system.

Other great merchants, whose names were towers of strength on 'change, were Goodhue, Aymar, Fish, King, Boorman, and Stewart. Henry Grinnell of Grinnell, Minturn & Co., became famous for his interest in arctic exploration, and in 1850 fitted out at his own expense an expedition to go in search of Sir John Franklin, which discovered and named after him Grinnells Land, in latitude $75° 24' 21''$ N.

The founders of these great houses were in almost all cases poor boys from the New England States or from foreign countries. So often was this the case that it was the subject of general remark. A shrewd observer, Walter Barrett, in his "Old Merchants of New York," thus wrote:

"It is a singular fact that a foreign-born boy or one from the New England States will succeed in this city and become a partner in our largest firms much oftener than a born New York boy. The great secret of their success is their perfect willingness to be useful and do what they are required to do, *and cheerfully*. Take, for instance, such a firm as Grinnell, Minturn & Co. In their countingroom they have New York boys and New England boys.

"Moses H. Grinnell comes down in the morning and says to John, a New York boy, 'John, take my overcoat up to my house in Fifth Avenue.' John takes the coat, mutters something about, 'I'm not an errand boy; I came here to learn the business,' and moves reluctantly. Mr. Grinnell sees it. At the same time one of his New England boys says, 'I'll take it up.' 'That's right; do so,' replies Mr. Grinnell, and to himself he says, 'That boy is smart, will work,' and he gives him plenty to do. Very soon he gets promoted, gains the confidence of the chief clerk and of his employers, and eventually gets into the firm as partner.

"It's so all over the city. It's so in every store, countingroom, and office. Outside boys get on faster than New York boys, owing to two reasons—they are not afraid to work, or to run of errands, or do cheerfully what they are told to do, and they do their work quickly."

There are golden grains of wisdom in the above for town boys and country boys alike.

## XXI. SHIPS AND SAILORS.

VERY soon after the centering in New York of the great highways described in a previous chapter, there were founded ocean lines to distribute throughout the known world the products they brought.

The first of these shipping enterprises of moment was the famous packet service between New York and Liverpool, England, founded in 1816 by five New York merchants—Isaac Wright & Son, Benjamin Marshall, Francis Thompson, and Jeremiah Thompson. Up to that date the merchantmen, which also carried passengers, were of French and British ownership, slow sailers, with dingy, shabby passenger appointments, and with no regular hour of sailing, leaving when loaded, or when wind and tide served. These men saw that ships unrivaled for size, strength, speed, and beauty, and sailing on a regular schedule would take the cream of the traffic, and founded the famous Black Ball line, still a fountain of happy memories to the old sea captains and merchants who haunt the docks and shipping offices about South Street and Burling Slip, or, safely moored in the Sailors' Snug Harbor, talk of past glories and adventures.

At first this line boasted but four ships, later increased to twelve, each a thing of beauty and an object of pride to the American heart. One of them sailed regularly on the 1st of every month. They were so successful that in 1821 a rival line, the Red Star, was established by Byrnes, Grimble & Co., with four ships, and sailing on the 24th of every month. To outdo them the Black Ball line added four new ships, and advertised a sailing on the 1st and 16th of every month. Then began an era of shipbuilding and mercantile expansion and competition such as the port had never seen.

Fish, Grinnell & Co. and Thaddeus Phelps & Co. soon founded the Swallowtail line, so called from its forked pennant, with departures on the 8th of every month, and New York papers proudly boasted of a weekly packet service to Liverpool. All these packets, you must understand, were gallant ships of from six hundred to fifteen hundred tons burden, and made the passage out from New York in twenty-three days, and the return in forty. Once the *Canada* of the Black Ball line broke the record by making the outward run in fifteen days and eighteen hours. In 1823 Grinnell, Minturn & Co. established a London line with sailings once a month. A line with four ships to Havre, France, was established about 1822 by Francis Depau.

These packets did much to build up the city by shortening and cheapening intercourse between her and European ports, and by driving the clumsy French and English traders from the seas they threw the carrying trade into American bottoms. They were also very profitable to their captains, agents, and builders, for each owned a share. By and by the rivalry became so keen that larger ships were built, the *Palestine* and

*Amazon*, of eighteen hundred tons each, being the largest as well as the last of their class. It is a tradition of South Street that the *Amazon* once made the voyage to Portsmouth, England, in fourteen days, a great feat for a sailing vessel, although the *Patrick*

A Clipper.

*Henry*, the *Montezuma*, the *Independence*, and the *Southampton* had performed the voyage to Liverpool in the same period.

But the packets were destined to be eclipsed in beauty and speed by a new model, also distinctly American—the clippers. These originated in Baltimore (according to some authorities; others say in New York) about 1840, in answer to a demand of the tea merchants for swift ships, even though of less carrying capacity. It was found that tea lost in flavor and other qualities with each additional day spent at sea; besides, a cargo was of such immense value that every day represented a large sum in interest and insurance—hence the demand for swift ships. The first clippers, built in New York by Smith & Dimon, were ordered by those famous China merchants, William H. Aspinwall, N. L. & G. Griswold, and A. A. Low & Brother, and were small, swift vessels of from six hundred to nine hundred tons burden.

The California gold excitement of 1849 created a demand for larger ships, and ushered in the golden age of the clippers. Provisions and machinery for the mines, passengers' baggage and outfits, were to be forwarded as far as San Francisco, half the distance to China, and created a demand for larger carrying capacity. New York shipbuilders were equal to the demand. The *Challenge* of 2,000 tons, the *Invincible* of 2,150 tons, the *Comet* of 1,209 tons, the *Sword Fish* of 1,150 tons, with the *Tornado*, the *Flying Cloud*, the *Black Squall*, and the *Sovereign of the Seas*, soon appeared, and were triumphs of the shipbuilder's art.

Mr. Sheldon, in an article on the old clippers in "Harper's Magazine" for January, 1884, has given so spirited an account of the exploits of these vessels that we cannot do better than quote an extract:

"That clipper epoch was an epoch to be proud of; and we were proud of it. The New York newspapers abounded in such headlines in large type as these: 'Quickest Trip on Record,' 'Shortest Passage to San Francisco,' 'Unparalleled Speed,' 'Quickest Voyage Yet,' 'A Clipper as is a Clipper,' 'Extraordinary

Dispatch,' 'The Quickest Voyage to China,' 'The Contest of the Clippers,' 'Great Passage from San Francisco,' 'Race Round the World.' The clipper ship *Surprise*, built in East Boston by Mr. Hall, and owned by A. A. Low & Brother, having sailed to San Francisco in ninety-six days, then the shortest time on record (Mr. W. H. Aspinwall's *Sea Witch* had run the course in ninety-seven days), a San Francisco journal said: 'One of our most distinguished merchants made a bet with a friend some weeks since that the *Surprise* would make the passage in ninety-six days, just the time she has consumed to a day. Yesterday morning, full of confidence, he mounted his old nag and rode over to the North Beach to get the first glimpse of the looked-for clipper. The fog, however, was rather thick outside, and after looking awhile he turned back to town, but had not arrived at his countingroom before he heard that the *Surprise* had passed the Golden Gate, and by eleven o'clock Captain Dumaresq was in his old friend's countingroom on Sansome Street. She has brought eighteen hundred tons of cargo, which may be estimated at a value of two hundred thousand dollars. Her manifest is twenty-five feet long.'

"Her greatest run was two hundred and eighty-four miles in twenty-four hours, and she reefed her topsails but twice during the voyage of 16,308 miles. She soon left San Francisco for London by way of Canton, and on reaching the English capital her receipts for freights had entirely paid her cost and running expenses, besides netting her owners a clear profit of fifty thousand dollars. At Canton her freight for London was engaged at six pounds sterling a ton, while the English ships were taking the same freight at three and four pounds a ton; and this was the second season that the preference had been given to American ships at advanced rates, their shorter passages enabling shippers to receive prompt returns from their investments, to save interest, and to secure an early market."

From this time (1850) until the Civil War, in 1860, swept American shipping from the seas, there were many famous contests between rival clippers. In 1850 the *Howqua*, Captain Daniel McKenzie, made the trip from Shanghai to New York in eighty-eight days. The *Samuel Russell*, on her homeward voyage from Whampoa, China, in 1851, made three hundred and eighteen miles in a single day,—thirteen and a quarter miles an hour,—a greater speed than any ocean steamer had at that time attained. For thirty days in succession she averaged two hundred and twenty-six miles a day. On another voyage to Canton she sailed three hundred and twenty-eight miles in one day, and on her return to New York reported her own arrival out at Canton. Both vessels were owned by A. A. Low & Brother of New York. The *Flying Cloud*, Captain Josiah P. Creesy, made the voyage to San Francisco in eighty-four days, distancing that of the *Surprise* by twelve days.

Such were some of the triumphs of American clippers a half century ago. Steamships, however, soon became formidable rivals, and with the invention of the screw propeller have nearly driven the clippers from the sea. Some of the former, with their exploits, it will be interesting to describe.

The first steamer to cross the Atlantic was an American vessel, the *Savannah*, which sailed from Savannah, Georgia, on May 26, 1819, for Liverpool, England. She was built in New York, having been launched in August, 1818, as a sailing packet to run between New York and Liverpool. As she came from the ways she was bought by several gentlemen of Savannah, and, at the suggestion of Captain Moses Rogers, fitted up as a steamer, with paddle wheels so contrived that they could be unshipped and shipped at pleasure. Her masts and rigging were retained, her owners not having full confidence in her ability to make her way wholly by steam.

She made her trial trip from New York to Savannah and back in April, 1819, using both steam and sail, and on her return to Savannah, in May of the same year, her owners determined to send her overseas to Liverpool. Her commander was Captain Moses Rogers, her navigator Stephen Rogers, both natives of New London, Connecticut. She carried in her bunkers seventy-five tons of coal and twenty-five cords of wood, and made the passage in twenty-six days—eight days under steam and eighteen under sail.

Stephen Rogers, her navigator, in a letter to the New London "Gazette," wrote that the *Savannah* was first sighted from the telegraph station at Cape Clear, on the southern coast of Ireland, which reported her as being on fire, whereupon the admiral sent a king's cutter to her relief. "But great was their wonder at their inability to come up with a ship under bare poles. After several shots had been fired from the cutter the engine was stopped, and the surprise of the cutter's crew at the mistake they had made, as well as their curiosity to see the strange Yankee craft, can be easily imagined."

As she steamed up the Mersey to Liverpool the wharves, shipping, and roofs of the houses were crowded with people, anxious to see the steamship that had crossed the ocean; and while she remained there she was visited by great crowds, including merchants and shipbuilders, who asked many questions as to her performances.

From Liverpool she proceeded to St. Petersburg, calling at Stockholm on her way, where she was visited by the King of Sweden, and also by "the American minister and lady, and all the foreign ministers and their ladies." She sailed from St. Petersburg on October 10, 1819, and reached Savannah on November 30 of the same year.

The results of her voyage did not encourage her owners to continue her as a steamship, however. Her boiler, engines, and paddles were removed, and she was placed on the Savannah route as a packet ship, and was finally wrecked on the Long Island coast.

Other successful attempts were made to cross the Atlantic by steam, but the cost was too great, and the "steam ferry" cannot be said to have been successfully established until the voyages of the *Sirius*, which sailed from Cork, Ireland, April 4, 1838, and reached New York on April 23; and of the *Great Western*, which sailed from Bristol, England, four days after the *Sirius*, and arrived in New York the same day, but a few hours later.

These boats belonged to rival companies, that had recently been formed to navigate the ocean by steam. The *Sirius* was sent out by the British and North American Company, which had been organized in London, only after great opposition from the owners of sailing vessels and others, by Dr. Junius Smith, an American scientist and inventor. This company forthwith contracted with Curling & Young of Blackwall for a "large and splendid steamship," the *British Queen*, of seventeen hundred tons burden, and designed expressly for the New York and London trade. Later her design was changed to twenty-four hundred tons.

Meantime a rival company, the Great Western Steamship Company, had been formed at the suggestion of Mr. Brussel, a famous engineer. This company began building the *Great Western*, of thirteen hundred and twenty tons, to ply between Bristol and New York. The *British Queen* was delayed by the nondelivery of her engines, and her owners, fearing that the rival company would send their *Great Western* first into the field and win the coveted honor of making the initial voyage across the Atlantic, chartered the *Sirius* and sent her out, with the result above described.

The *British Queen* was finally completed, and made her maiden voyage in July, 1839, crossing from London to New York in fourteen and a half days without mishap or detention. The success of these steamers led the companies which owned them to build others, and soon there were lines of steamers leaving New York and London or Liverpool regularly. A prospectus of the British and American Steam Navigation Company issued in the summer of 1838 assured the public that in 1839 they would be able to dispatch steamers for New York on the 1st and 16th of each month from London and Liverpool alternately.

In 1839–1840 Samuel Cunard, an enterprising merchant of Halifax, Nova Scotia, founded the famous Cunard line, which has been in steady operation ever since, dispatching vessels regularly from New York, Boston, and Halifax.

## XXII. NEW YORK IN THE CIVIL WAR.

THROUGH the exciting days of 1860-1861, when war and rumors of war filled the air, the voice of New York was for peace. A commercial community, she was naturally conservative, and averse to a change. War would destroy her commerce. Debts to the amount of millions of dollars were due her from Southern merchants. War would confiscate every dollar. Naturally, as the great conflict drew near, her merchants made the most serious efforts to ward it off. On January 12, 1861, a memorial signed by hundreds of her business men was sent to Congress, praying that the pending troubles might be settled by peaceful means. On the 18th another memorial of the same tenor, with forty thousand names attached, was indorsed at a meeting held in the Chamber of Commerce, and forwarded to Washington. Later a mass meeting was held in Cooper Institute, at which three delegates were appointed to confer with representatives of the six States that had already seceded, with a view to healing the breach by concession and compromise. At the same meeting, with the same object, a Peace Society was formed, with the venerable Professor S. F. B. Morse, the inventor of the telegraph, as president.

Then came April 12, 1861. The old flag was fired

on at Fort Sumter, and fell dishonored before the palmetto standard. In a moment the current of popular feeling in New York changed. Self-interest withered. Patriotism revived and became uppermost. Democrats vied with Republicans in sentiments of loyalty to the flag. Eight days after, at a great mass meeting held in Union Square, Fernando Wood, then mayor, in an eloquent speech, declared that "the Union must and shall be preserved," notwithstanding that the January previous he had sent a message to the common council proposing that the city of New York herself secede from the rest of the State. The air was electric with military ardor and patriotic enthusiasm. Regiments mustered in their armories, or marched through the streets to the sound of drum, fife, and bugle, on their way to the front. The great poet of the city, Bryant, expressed the feeling of all when he wrote:

> "Lay down the ax, fling by the spade,
> Leave in its track the toiling plow:
> The rifle and the bayonet blade
> For arms like yours are fitter now.
> And let the hands that ply the pen
> Quit the light task, and learn to wield
> The horseman's crooked brand, and rein
> The charger on the battlefield."

On the 18th of April, 1861, the gallant Sixth Massachusetts marched through the city on its way to the imperiled capital, and added to the excitement. The Rev. Dr. Dix, an eyewitness, thus described the attendant scenes:

"They came in at night, and it was understood that

after breakfast at the Astor House the march would be resumed. By nine next morning an immense crowd had assembled about the hotel. Broadway from Barclay to Fulton Street, and the lower end of Park Row, were occupied by a dense mass of human beings, all watching the front entrance, at which the regiment was to file out. From side to side, from wall to wall, extended that innumerable host, silent as the grave, expectant, something unspeakable in their faces. It was the dread, deep hush before the thunderstorm. At last a low murmur was heard; it sounded somewhat like the gasp of men in suspense, and the cause was that the soldiers had appeared, their leading files descending the steps. By the twinkle of their bayonets above the heads of the crowd their course could be traced out into the open street in front. Formed at last in column they stood, the band at the head, and the word was given, 'March.' Still a dead silence prevailed. Then the drums rolled out the time, the regiment was in motion, and then the band, bursting into full volume, struck up—what other tune could the Massachusetts men have chosen?—'Yankee Doodle.'

"I caught about two bars and a half of the old tune, not more, for instantly there rose a sound such as many a man never heard in his life, and never will hear, such as is never heard more than once in a lifetime. Not more awful is the thunder of heaven, as with solemn peal it smites into silence all lesser sounds, and rolling through the vault above us, fills earth and sky with the shock of its terrible voice. One terrific roar burst from the multitude, leaving nothing audible save its own reverberation. We saw the heads of armed men, the gleam of their weapons, the regimental colors, all moving on pageantlike, but naught could we hear save that one hoarse, heavy surge, one general acclaim, one wild shout of joy and hope, one endless cheer, rolling up and down, from side to side, above, below, to right, to left

Departure of the Seventh Regiment, 1861.

—the voice of approval, of consent, of unity in act and will. No one who saw and heard could doubt how New York was going."

The famous Seventh Regiment, the pride of New York, was but a few hours behind, marching at 3 P. M. on the 19th, nine hundred and ninety-one men strong. "Was there ever such an ovation?" wrote the poet and soldier Fitz-James O'Brien, who was one of them.

"The marble walls of Broadway were never before rent with such cheers as greeted us when we passed. The façades of the buildings were so thick with people that it seemed as if an army of black ants were marching, after their resistless fashion, through the city, and had scaled the houses. Handkerchiefs fluttered in the air like myriads of white butterflies. An avenue of brave, honest faces smiled upon us as we passed, and sent a sunshine into our hearts that lives there still."

Next day the Sixth, Twelfth, and Seventy-first embarked for Washington by way of Fortress Monroe, to avoid Baltimore, where the Massachusetts men had met resistance, and on April 23 the Eighth, Thirteenth, Twenty-eighth, and Sixty-ninth took up the line of march.

Meantime the city authorities and the citizens had not been idle. The common council appropriated one million dollars to aid in carrying on the war. Generous private subscriptions were given to equip and care for the soldiers. Thirteen banks in New York alone gave nearly one million dollars. In ten days New York city sent eight thousand men to the front.

To care for these troops and their families, defend the city, and aid the government, a Union Defense Committee was soon organized, with the Hon. John A. Dix, who had been a member of President Buchanan's cabinet, as chairman. This committee during the war aided in organizing and equipping forty-nine regiments, containing some forty thousand men, and disbursed a million dollars in aiding the city's soldiers and their families.

The loyal women of the city, not to be outdone by their brothers, organized, in 1861, a Woman's Central Relief Association, which soon had branches in all of the Northern States. The ladies, however, found that they needed government aid and sanction to render their society effective, and at their request Secretary of War Stanton created the United States Sanitary Commission, "for inquiry and advice in respect to the sanitary needs of the United States forces." This commission comprised six competent gentlemen, with the Rev. Henry W. Bellows, a famous Unitarian clergyman of New York, as president, and under its authority the ladies, with rare energy and enthusiasm, worked. It is said that the New York branch collected and sent to the army during the four years of war fifteen million dollars' worth of supplies and five million dollars in money. The same year, following the suggestion of Mr. Vincent Colyer, a well-known artist, the Christian Commission was organized in New York, to attend to the moral and spiritual welfare of the soldiers. Shortly before this Miss Dorothéa L. Dix had offered her services to the government as a nurse in the hospitals, and became the head of the American Order of Florence Nightingales, a body of devoted women, who served their country quite as faithfully by loving and gratuitous service in the hospitals as did their brothers on the field.

In May, 1863, there came sad reverses to the Union arms. Hooker had been defeated by Lee at Chancellorsville, and the latter had carried the war into Africa by invading Pennsylvania. To fill up our decimated armies, President Lincoln, the same month, ordered a draft of three hundred thousand men. There was at this time a great body of evil-disposed men in New York, with whom the war was unpopular, and who had sworn to resist such a draft if ordered. This the State and city authorities knew perfectly well, but no steps seem to have been taken to guard against such an uprising; instead the city as well as the State militia was hurried off to swell the armies confronting Lee. Only the police force, a handful of regulars, and a few members of the invalid corps were left. The draft was ordered for Saturday, July 11, 1863, and began in the Eleventh and Ninth districts, without disturbance of any sort. Next day, Sunday, seems to have been used to foment trouble.

On Monday morning the wheel was set in motion at the enrolling offices at 677 Third Avenue and 1190 Broadway, and the draft continued until noon, when it was stopped because of disturbances in the city. At about ten o'clock that morning John A. Kennedy, superintendent of police, was set upon by the rioters at the corner of Lexington Avenue and Forty-sixth Street, and would probably have been beaten to death but for the aid of an influential friend. Almost instantly the mob grew to threatening proportions, and surrounded the Police Headquarters on Mulberry Street in a menacing way. President Acton at once took command, and by telegraph called out the entire police force, which assembled at its respective station houses, and for three days struggled with the greatly superior forces of the mob. Third Avenue at this time, from Cooper Institute to Forty-sixth Street, was black with human beings. Many other streets presented a similar appearance. Small bodies of police, when encountered, were driven off or trampled under foot. Growing bolder, the rioters broke open stores, fired houses, and inaugurated a carnival of crime.

The negroes they hated especially, because they considered that they were the cause of the war. These, wherever found, whether men, women, or children, were seized and hanged to the nearest lamp-posts. By and by a large body of the rioters swooped down upon the Colored Orphan Asylum, on Fifth Avenue, between Forty-

The Draft Riot.

third and Forty-fourth streets. Two hundred helpless children were gathered there, but while the mob was breaking in the front doors, they were hurried out by the rear, and found safety in neighboring houses. The rioters, finding that their prey had escaped, applied the torch to the house in twenty places at once, and burned it to the ground.

Five thousand men now set out for Police Headquarters, breathing threats of slaughter against the police. To meet them President Acton detailed two hundred men, under Sergeant Daniel Carpenter, who proved himself an able commander as well as a brave soldier. Sending detachments up the parallel streets, he led a column down Bleecker Street to Broadway, and charged the mob in front, while the detachments took them in flank and rear, and scattered them like chaff.

That night it became evident that the situation was critical, and Mayor Opdyke called on General Wool, commanding the regulars, for aid, and also on General Sandford, commanding the State National Guard. Wool detailed Colonel Harvey Brown, of the Fifth Artillery, with all the men he could muster, who took post at Police Headquarters, while General Sandford, with seven hundred men, occupied the State Arsenal, on the corner of Seventh Avenue and Thirty-fifth Street.

For two days the mob, met by the bullets and bayonets of the troops, fought and gave way, or scattered and extended the region of disturbance northward to Harlem and westward to Sixth Avenue. There were many hand-to-hand conflicts, but at length, on the third day, the force being increased by the ordering home of the city regiments, discipline prevailed, and at midnight the telegraph reported all quiet.

One thousand of the rioters had been killed and many more wounded.

In the spring of 1865 an ovation to the veterans, who returned with tattered banners and honorable scars, closed the record of the Civil War.

## XXIII. AN OLD MAN'S RECOLLECTIONS OF NEW YORK.

SOMETIMES we have the pleasure of strolling along Broadway with a highly respected friend, an old gentleman of eighty-five, who is still alert and vigorous, and brimming over with recollections of old times, when he was young.

"Strange," said he, one morning, "but the most vivid of my boyhood impressions are of the Broadway stages, which were first put on about 1830. Four fine horses drew them, and there was a Jehu above who knew how to handle the ribbons. All the stages were painted in the brightest colors, and properly named as 'Lady Clinton,' 'Lady Washington,' 'The Knickerbocker,' etc. They left the Battery hourly for Greenwich, Harlem, Bloomingdale, and Manhattanville, and no fare was collected till the end of the route. I seem to hear this moment the drivers calling, 'Manhattanville, ma'm,' 'Right away for Yorkville,' and so on.

"Down there at the corner of West Broadway and Franklin was Riley's Fifth Ward Museum Hotel, the Eden Musée of my youthful days. On its walls, and in glass cases, were original portraits of great warriors and statesmen, decorated with their swords and portions of their uniforms. There were also curiosities—a two-

Broadway Stages.

headed calf, a pig that had killed a man by butting him off a bridge, one of the Hawaiian clubs that had dashed out the brains of Captain Cook, General Jackson's pipe, Tecumseh's rifle, and many relics of colonial days in New York.

"What interested us boys most, because it brought back the days of the Revolution, was a headless and armless statue of William Pitt, the very one that the patriots of New York raised on the steps of the Royal Exchange, in 1766, to celebrate the repeal of the Stamp Act, and which British soldiers mutilated in the war, because the patriots had carried off the leaden statue of George III., which stood on the Bowling Green, and melted it up for bullets. Over there on the Hudson, at the foot of the present Houston Street, was a great swamp, where I've roosted pigeons many a time, and Minetta Brook, that flowed through it—never were there such trout as I caught there in my schoolboy days."

When we came to Canal Street my friend looked up and down its wide vista longingly.

"Here I lived as a boy," he said at last. "It was the

Canal Street and Broadway.

fashionable street of the city in 1820-1830. Beginning in 1809, a canal was dug through the marshes to the North River, for draining the great pond, called the Collect, on the present site of the Tombs. A street was laid out on each side of this canal, with a double row of beautiful shade trees, the whole forming a noble thoroughfare one hundred feet wide, the present Canal Street. Many of the old Knickerbocker families settled there, the lawns of their fine mansions extending to the street, and their flower and vegetable gardens, pastures and meadows, stretching back into the country. We boys had our canoes on the canal in summer and skated there in winter. It seems as though there are no such maidens nowadays as sailed and skated with us on that dear old canal."

Here our venerable friend paused and looked through the maze of buildings toward the southeast.

"Down there," said he, "where the hide and leather men now have their mart, lay another great swamp in my father's day. In the rear of the Harpers' great establishment, he told me, he had often shot duck and trapped mink and otter.

"In 1825, while I was still a boy, it was all open country above Astor Place—forest and swamp, farms and farmhouses, apple orchards and gardens. On the present site of Grace Church stood a high, peaked barn, and above it, up to the powder house (now Union Square), were but two dwellings—old stone farmhouses with long, sloping roofs and dormer windows. A little south of the present site of the Astor Library were the Vauxhall Gardens, reaching through from Broadway to the Bowery, and beautifully laid out with flowers, lawns, trees, and shrubbery, where a band played on summer nights, and polite New York, as well as the commonalty, came to see the fireworks and to partake of ice cream, cakes, and ale. Farther north, in the apex of the triangle made by the junction of Third and Fourth avenues, stood Peter Cooper's grocery store, on the site of the present Cooper Institute, and many a penny have I exchanged there for the seductive jackson ball or taffy.

"Bleecker Street was my great blackberry preserve when a boy. What luscious berries grew beside its walls, and wild roses—none such bloom nowadays."

Another day we began at the City Hall, and went for a stroll down Broadway to the Battery, and around by the East River docks, where the few sailing ships that remain are moored.

"The City Hall," he began, "was opened in 1812, having been nine years in building. That was one year before I was born. It stood between two prisons, I remember, the Bridewell and the jail. On the north side of the park, on Chambers Street, were the Academy of Fine Arts, founded in 1808, with Chancellor Livingston as president, and the famous painter John Trumbull as vice president, and the almshouse. A space farther east was the Rotunda of John Vanderlyn, where people went to see pictures as now they go to the National Academy or Fine Arts Building. Vanderlyn was a notable artist in my day, and one of the pets of society. His 'Marius amid the Ruins of Carthage' had taken the prize at the Paris Salon, and he returned to New York a famous man. To encourage art the city built the Rotunda, and gave Vanderlyn the lease of it for a studio and for the exhibition of his pictures.

"On the southeast side of the park, near the site of the present 'Sun' building, stood the old Park Theater, the fashionable place of amusement of my day, where I saw Edmund Kean and Charles Mathews and other actors, and such assemblages of fair women and brave men as are rarely seen nowadays. This theater was burned on the morning of May 25, 1820, but John Jacob

Astor and John K. Beckman rebuilt it on the old site in much handsomer style.

"Tammany Hall then stood on the east side of the park, at the corner of Frankfort Street. Aaron Burr, who returned to New York quietly in 1812, and in a week held retainers to the amount of twenty thousand

Tammany Hall.

dollars, had an office in the hall, and was understood to be one of its ruling spirits.

"The south side of the park was then for the most part covered with low wooden buildings, in which were cigar stores, fruit shops, beer saloons, and the like. The present giants of the press that later took possession of so large a space of it were then unknown. I have seen them grow from infancy. The 'Sun' was founded first, in 1833, next the 'Herald' in 1835, the 'Tribune' in 1841, the 'Times' in 1851, and the 'World' in 1860.

"Lower Broadway," my friend continued, "was in my day almost as crowded and noisy as now. I saw traffic blocked at the corner of Fulton and Broadway in boyhood, and the policemen stationed there were kept quite as busy then as now.

"The street venders were almost as numerous then, too, but of a different character. Some sold hot corn on the ear; some sold baked pears swimming in molasses; others, in long white frocks, peddled Rockaway sand in two-wheeled carts. Colored men hawked bundles of straw for filling beds, and an old blind man sold door mats made of picked tarred rope. There were men who made fortunes by supplying the people with 'tea water' at two cents a pail, from clear, cold springs in the upper part of the island. Before Croton water came in 1842, you know, we were dependent for water on wells, cisterns, and springs.

"We had bogy men, too, that our mothers and nurses frightened us with, just as now they use the sandman. There was the 'limekiln man,' so called because he slept in the limekilns around Gansevoort Street, and went about in shabby clothes white with lime, forever muttering to himself. There was the 'blue man,' with face bluish in color, and a man who in the coldest weather walked the streets without an overcoat."

By this time we had arrived at the Battery.

"I am rejoiced," said he, "to see this park of my boyhood reclaimed and made once more a beautiful place. In my day it was the fashionable promenade of the city. The old fort, which, I see, they have uncovered and turned into an aquarium, then pointed grim guns seaward through its embrasures. We called it Fort Clinton. It was built about 1807, when our troubles with England and France pointed to war; and when war with England finally came in 1812, it formed one of the defenses of the city. Later it was turned into a

Castle Garden

summer resort, called Castle Garden, with concerts and other attractions. I heard Jenny Lind there in 1850, when she made her first appearance in America under the auspices of the great P. T. Barnum. It was on Wednesday, September 11, and four thousand people crowded into the garden to hear her sing.

"It is historic ground, this Battery. From it the British took their departure in 1783, and Washington set out for Paulus Hook on his way to Virginia, and here we received Lafayette on his second visit to this country in 1824. Lafayette arrived on the French packet *Cadmus* from Havre, and was met down the harbor by the city fathers, with our handsome and scholarly mayor, William Paulding, at their head. Next day the city held a holiday in his honor. At nine in the morning the city officials, the Chamber of Commerce, and the Society of the Cincinnati proceeded to Staten Island, where Lafayette had spent the night as the guest of Vice President Daniel D. Tompkins, and escorted to New York the man whom the whole country delighted to honor, because he had fought for her in the Revolution, and had later performed great services for liberty and humanity in his own country.

"The brilliant company landed here at a carpeted stairway, over which rose an arch decorated with laurel and the flags of all nations. I saw Lafayette, a small, delicate man, with fine, clear-cut features and the erect and martial air of the soldier, and I can hear again the salvos of artillery and the cheers of thousands that greeted him as he set foot on the stairway. After saluting the people in return he entered a carriage, to which four horses were attached, and was driven to the City Hall, where he was formally welcomed by Mayor Paulding."

During another stroll my friend spoke of the improvements and inventions he had seen come into use. Gas, street cars, Croton water, the elevated road, telephone, district messenger service, parks, elevators—he had seen them all.

"People began talking about gas in 1817," he said. "It had been used by David Murdoch to light a house in Redruth, Cornwall, England, as early as 1792, but came into use slowly. The first mains were laid in Broadway in 1825. Before that we used tallow dips and whale oil lamps. I well remember how timid people hesitated about allowing the mysterious new agent to come into their houses. Up to 1852, nine years before the war, we had no street cars, only stages and omnibuses. There were twenty-four lines of these in 1851. The first street car line opened was the Sixth Avenue, in 1852, and so great a convenience did it prove that they rapidly multiplied. The elevated roads did not begin running until 1876, the Ninth Avenue line being completed that year as far as Fifty-ninth Street. In June, 1878, the Sixth Avenue line was opened from Rector Street to Central Park; in August of the same year the Third Avenue line was opened to Forty-second Street; and in 1880 the Second Avenue line to Sixty-seventh Street. The same year the lines on both sides of the city reached Harlem.

"Croton water dates only from 1842. An agitation for pure water began in 1831. Up to that time we had used water from wells and springs, which, with the growth of the city, began to be rendered impure by sewage, and produced much sickness. Many men turned an honest penny by bringing water in carts from the upper part of the island. Robert L. Stevens, a famous engineer of that day, was, I believe, the first to suggest the Croton watershed for a supply. A large party was in favor of the Bronx. Many surveys were made, many plans broached and discussed. At last a board of engineers reported in favor of an aqueduct fifteen miles long to take Croton water near the mouth of that river, and deliver thirty million gallons daily at a distributing reservoir on Murray Hill.

"The legislature ordered a vote of the people to decide whether this should be done, and as this was overwhelmingly in favor, the engineers at once began the stupendous work. Croton Lake was first staked out, and the course of the aqueduct from the dam to the Harlem laid out. At this point Major David B. Douglas, the engineer in charge, had a difficulty with the chairman of the board of commissioners, and was retired, John B. Jervis, an engineer and inventor of merit, who had assisted in building the Erie Canal, being appointed in his place; but Major Douglas's plans were retained. For several years the great work went on section after section being completed, the legislature authorizing the money to pay for each as it was finished. A dam was thrown across the Croton, deep ravines were crossed, lofty hills tunneled, an aqueduct bridge across the deep valley of Sing Sing built, and another, the present High Bridge, over the Harlem. On June 22, 1842, the work was practically complete from the Croton to the distributing reservoir at Fifth Avenue and Forty-second Street, except that, High Bridge not being finished, the water was carried for the time being by siphon pipes under the Harlem River.

"On June 22 water was for the first time let into the canal, and a small boat, called the *Croton Maid*, carrying four persons, was sent through it. On June 27 water was admitted to the receiving reservoir at Yorkville in the presence of the governor of the State, the mayor, common council, and many other dignitaries of the city, and on July 4, with similar ceremonies, to the distributing reservoir.

"On the succeeding 14th of October the people celebrated the event. New York had never seen such a splendid pageant, which far surpassed, it is said, that at the opening of the Erie Canal in 1825. The governor and other State officers, members of Congress, foreign consuls, mayors of other cities, were present, and took part in the great parade, which stretched from one end of the city to the other. At the City Hall President

City Hall Park.

Stevens made a formal transfer of the aqueduct to the city, artillery thundered in honor of the event, and the new fountain in City Hall Park sent its pearly column sixty feet into the air.

"You can scarcely believe that until 1857, four years before the Civil War, we had no parks worthy of the name, the Battery and City Hall Park being really the city's only breathing places. In 1853, as a result of two years' agitation, the legislature authorized the city to take the land between Fifty-ninth and One Hundred and Sixth streets and Fifth and Eighth avenues for a public park; later the northern line was extended to One Hundred and Tenth Street. The tract was then a wilderness of crag, swamp, pestilential pool, and rocky ravine, covered with unsightly hovels, stables, and other nuisances. On April 17, 1857, an act passed the legislature which named the proposed new park Central Park, and created a board of eleven commissioners for laying it out. This board advertised for plans, and from the thirty-three submitted chose that of two young landscape architects, Frederick Law Olmsted and Calvert Vaux, as the best. Their plan provided for a broad driveway so constructed as to make as long and beautiful a road as possible, winding in and out amid lakes, forests, glens, cascades, meadows, and pastures. A small army of workmen was engaged, and, under the leadership of the two gentlemen above named, converted the unsightly waste into the beautiful earthly paradise we now know.

"Riverside Park was acquired 1869–1872, and Morningside Park soon after. But the city was now fully alive to the beauty and necessity of these breathing places, and in 1883, soon after the annexation of the Westchester County towns, the legislature appointed a commission to secure lands for public parks above the Harlem. This commission reported in 1884, and the legislature then provided for the laying out of Van Cortlandt, Bronx, Pelham Bay, Crotona, Claremont, and St. Marys parks, which, with their connecting parkways, stretch from the Hudson to the Sound,[1] and give New York a system of public parks equaled by no other city in the world."

[1] For a fuller description of these parks see Chapter XXVII.

# XXIV. A HUNDRED YEARS OF PROGRESS.

WHEN the British left New York in 1783, a line drawn from Catherine Street, on the East River, across the island to the foot of Reade Street, on the Hudson, would have inclosed the city. The streets were

Oldtime Mansion, Washington Square.

irregular, the houses of red brick, mostly with tiled and pointed roofs. Wall Street was wide and elegant. Broadway was the fashionable quarter. In 1795 sewers were first introduced. In 1800 the town boasted sixty thousand inhabitants. By 1825 the city had reached

Bleecker Street. In 1843-1844, after the introduction of Croton water, a new era of progress began. Fashionable New York escaped from its modest dwellings downtown, and began to build houses of far greater pretension uptown. Some of these mansions you may still see in Washington Square, Waverley Place, Bond Street, and lower Fifth Avenue, which then became the fashionable quarter. Shrewd observers now noted in the people a much nearer approach to the European

"Brownstone began to be used."

style of living. "The number of servants in livery increases," wrote Lydia Maria Child, the poetess, about this time. "Foreign artistic upholsterers are being imported. There will soon be more houses furnished according to the taste and fashion of noblemen in New York than in Paris. Furniture for a single room often costs ten thousand dollars."

By 1850 the city had reached Thirty-fourth Street on the north, and covered the ground from river to river. Yorkville, Bloomingdale, and Manhattanville were still lovely pastoral villages in the open country. By 1856 the population had reached six hundred and thirty thousand. Brownstone instead of red brick began to be used for building about this time. People lived in their own houses, and not in apartments or hotels. Tenements were few, and French flats wholly unknown. The streets were badly paved and lighted, and, being rarely cleaned, emitted the odors of the streets of Cologne. New York was metropolitan only in its commerce. This state of affairs continued until 1865.

A Scene on Broadway, 1893.

During the war New York made little progress, but with the return of peace she awoke from her slumbers, and entered upon an era of enterprise that in a generation transformed her into a metropolis. In 1865 the country above Forty-second Street was a wilderness of forest and crag, of ungraded and unpaved streets, with the squatter's cabin perched on every available eminence. Rapid transit being then unknown, and street cars few, people could not reach the upper part of the island, and New York expanded in the direction of Brooklyn, New Jersey, and Staten Island. In 1865 there was scarcely a six-story building in the city. The Astor House was one of the most notable structures,

The Brooklyn Bridge.

and was the most elegant hotel in New York. Most of the houses were two and three stories high, but the invention of the elevator made the present towering structures possible.

The demand for cheaper homes and rents led also to the building of the East River Bridge, a company to build it being incorporated by the legislature in 1867, with John A. Roebling as chief engineer. In January, 1870, work was begun on the foundations for the towers.

Wall Street.

John A. Roebling, the great engineer, died before his grand conception was realized, and his equally gifted son, Washington A. Roebling, took up the work and carried it to completion. The bridge was completed and dedicated with appropriate ceremonies on May 24, 1883, thirteen years after the work began.

Meantime New York was pushing her way northward toward the Harlem. The first ten years after the war were marked by reckless speculation, especially in real estate, a mania greatly stimulated by the Tweed Ring,[1] which came into power during this period.

[1] This ring was formed by William M. Tweed, a politician of the city, who, after filling various minor offices, became chairman of the board of supervisors and deputy street commissioner, an office which put him in control of the city's public works. The ring's methods were simple but shrewd: for everything done for or furnished to the city a sum ranging from sixty to eighty-five per cent more than the real cost was charged in the

In 1870 New York had 64,044 houses and 942,292 inhabitants. The desire for expansion and the certainty of rapid transit by the elevated railroads led to the annexation in 1873 of the three towns of Morrisania, West Farms, and Kingsboro, in Westchester County, above the Harlem, which movement carried the city's northerly boundary line to Yonkers, and added thirteen thousand acres to her area. By act of the legislature of 1895 Westchester, Eastchester, Pelham, and Wakefield (South Mount Vernon) were annexed, adding twenty thousand acres more, and carrying her boundary line eastward to the city of Mount Vernon.

bills, the excess being divided among the members of the ring. Tweed added to the prevailing mania by projecting public improvements of every sort on a large scale. Detection and punishment came to the conspirators at last. In 1871 copies of the fraudulent bills came into possession of the New York "Times," which gave them to the public in double-leaded columns. Other members of the press ably seconded the "Times," and a committee of seventy was formed to bring the rogues to justice. Most of the latter fled to Europe. Tweed remained, was arrested, tried, and sentenced to the penitentiary on Blackwells Island, from which, in 1875, his friends procured his release on bail; but he was at once re-arrested on a civil suit to recover six million dollars alleged to have been stolen from the city treasury. Not being able to find the bail required,— three million dollars,— he was lodged in Ludlow Street Jail, whence he shortly after escaped and fled to Spain. The Spanish authorities delivered him up at our request, however; he was brought back, tried on the civil suit, and a verdict of $6,537,000 returned against him by the jury. Being unable to pay this, he was thrown into jail, and there died in January, 1878.

## XXV. GREATER NEW YORK.

IT would be difficult to decide who first publicly advocated a union of New York with Brooklyn and neighboring towns on Long Island and above the Harlem. Ex-Comptroller Andrew H. Green, because of his earnest and persistent advocacy of it, has been called the father of the movement. Practically the interests of these towns and of New York were the same, and it was believed that with a wider territory government would be less costly, and the formation of rings and cliques to control patronage would be more difficult. The question first took tangible shape when the legislature of New York, in 1890, created a commission "to inquire into the expediency of the proposed consolidation, and to submit a report with recommendations." Andrew H. Green of New York was president of this commission, and J. S. T. Stranahan of Brooklyn vice president; there were also nine other members, chosen impartially from the cities and towns interested.

This commission presented a bill to the legislature of 1893, submitting the question to a plebiscite, or vote of the people of the districts interested. The bill was not acted on at that time, however, but the next legislature —that of 1894—passed it, and the people, when the question came before them, voted in favor of it, that is, all except the city of Mount Vernon, the town of Westchester, and the township of Flushing. To the legislature of 1895 the commission presented a report, and with it a bill declaring the districts affected—with the

Wharves, East Shore of Manhattan.

exception of Mount Vernon—a part of the city of New York. But the bill failed to pass, because of the adoption of an amendment, at the closing hours of the session, referring the whole matter back to the people. As a result of the movement, however, the legislature at this session annexed the towns of Westchester, Eastchester, Pelham, and some other parts of Westchester County to New York. But the matter was not allowed to rest.

The legislature of 1896 appointed a joint committee of four senators and five assemblymen to inquire into the matter and report not later than March 11, 1896. This committee, through its chairman, Senator Lexow, reported in favor of consolidation, and also a bill to effect it, which bill passed the Senate by a vote of thirty-eight to eight, and the Assembly by a vote of ninety-one to fifty-six, and this despite strenuous opposition by prominent citizens of New York and Brooklyn. It was then submitted, according to law, to the mayors of New York, Brooklyn, and Long Island City (the cities interested), was vetoed by Mayor Strong of New York and by Mayor Wurster of Brooklyn, and approved by Mayor Gleason of Long Island City. The measure then went back to the Assembly, and was a second time passed over the vetoes of the two mayors, and was signed by Governor Morton on May 11, 1896, thus becoming a law. Section 1 of this act defined the bounds of the territory to be added to New York, viz., the county of Kings

Hotel Waldorf-Astoria, New York.

(Brooklyn), the county of Richmond (Staten Island), the city of Long Island City, the towns of Newtown, Flushing, Jamaica, and that part of the town of Hempstead which is westerly of a straight line drawn from the southeasterly point of the town of Flushing, through the middle of the channel between Rockaway Beach and Shelter Island, to the Atlantic Ocean.

Section 3 provided for a commission of fifteen persons,—the president of the commission of 1890, the mayors of New York, Brooklyn, and Long Island City, the State engineer, surveyor, and attorney-general, and nine other persons,—to be appointed by the governor, to draft a charter or form of government for the enlarged city. This commission, of which Benjamin F. Tracy was president and George M. Pinney, Jr., secretary, submitted a charter for the greater city to the legislature of 1897, which, after amendments by that body, was adopted and approved by Governor Black May 2, 1897.

As citizens of New York we are interested in this charter, which prescribes the government under which we shall live, no doubt, for many years. By examining it closely we shall see that it differs considerably from former charters. One great point of difference is that it adopts the borough system of government, after the English fashion. There are five of these boroughs, viz., the borough of Manhattan, which includes the old city of New York, on Manhattan Island and the adjacent islands; the borough of the Bronx, which includes the annexed district above the Harlem and Spuyten Duyvil Creek, and the islands adjacent; the borough of Brooklyn, comprising the whole of Kings County; the borough of Queens, including that part of Queens County named in the act of annexation; and the borough of Richmond, which comprises all of Staten Island.

The government is vested in a mayor and a municipal assembly of two chambers—a council composed of twenty-nine members, who are elected for four years, and a board of aldermen of sixty members, who are elected for two years. The president of the council is elected by the entire city, but the other twenty-eight members are chosen by districts. There are five of these districts in the boroughs of Manhattan and the Bronx, each of which chooses three councilmen, and three in the borough of Brooklyn, which choose the same number, while the boroughs of Queens and of Richmond are each represented by two members.

The aldermen are chosen by assembly districts, each of the sixty assembly districts of the city sending one member. Ex-mayors of the new city will have a seat in the council, but no vote, and the heads of departments seats in the board of aldermen, with the same restriction.

The municipal assembly wields large powers, subject to certain checks and restrictions. It has power to establish ferries and to build tunnels under and bridges over all waters within the city limits, to build docks and improve the water front, to open and extend streets, construct parks, schoolhouses, and public buildings, and supply water and the means of rapid transit from one quarter of the city to another; but its acts are subject to the approval of the mayor, and to pass a grant of any public franchise over his veto it must have a five-sixths vote. In granting franchises the approval of the board of estimate and apportionment is also required. The grant, if of a street or highway, can be for only twenty-five years. The Assembly cannot authorize loans or issue bonds without the prior approval of the above-named board, and if such bond issue is for repaving streets it must be unanimous. It may also establish additional waterworks and acquire property for the purpose. It must consider the yearly tax budget when prepared by the board of estimate and apportionment, and may reduce it, but cannot increase it. It has power to pass all necessary laws and ordinances, and must see that these are faithfully observed. Contracts for city work or supplies of more than one thousand dollars' value must be authorized by this assembly unless it otherwise orders by a three-fourths vote.

The business of the city is carried on by the mayor and his heads of departments. The mayor is elected for a term of four years by the whole city, and appoints all heads of departments, except the comptroller, who is elected by the people. There are fourteen departments,—finance, law, police, public improvements, bridges, parks, buildings, public charities, correction, fire, docks and ferries, taxes and assessments, education, and health,—besides six included in the department of public works, viz., water supply, highways, street cleaning, sewers, public buildings, lighting and supplies.

The department of public works is a very important one. It is composed of the heads of the six departments above enumerated, together with a president of the board (who is appointed by the mayor). The mayor, comptroller, corporation counsel, and the presidents of the five boroughs are members of it by virtue of their office, but the presidents can vote only upon questions affecting their respective boroughs. This board has charge of all the streets, bridges, and the sewer and water systems of the city. It must take the first step in all proposed public improvements, but if the work be of great extent it must also have the approval of the board of estimate and apportionment. All work ordered by it must have the approval of the municipal assembly. This board, in addition to its other powers, may lay out new streets and parks, build new bridges and tunnels and their approaches, change the grades of streets, and so forth.

Another very important board is that of estimate and apportionment, which is composed of the mayor, comptroller, corporation counsel, president of the council, and president of the board of taxes and assessments. Its principal duty is, before January 1 of each year, to make a "budget," or estimate of the amount of money required to conduct the business of the city during the ensuing year. It must also provide money to meet the city's obligations, or bonds, as they become due, and pay the interest on the same; also audit charges against the city for counsel's fees incurred by city officials in defending themselves against unjust charges; fix, with the municipal assembly, the salaries of certain employees, transfer excess of appropriations from one department to another, and perform various other minor duties.

The borough boards form the most novel feature of the new charter. These boards consist of a president, who is elected by the people of the borough for a term of four years, and the members of the municipal assembly residing within the borough limits. Each borough is divided into districts of local improvement, which are the same as the Senate districts of the counties; then each of these districts has its local board, composed of the members of the municipal assembly residing in that district. These local boards have power to begin proceedings in all cases of street or sewer improvement within their district, where the work is to be paid for in whole or in part by assessments on the property of that district. They can also recommend the laying of sidewalks and the providing of street lamps and signs. They also hear complaints of nuisances in streets, or of disorderly houses, liquor saloons, gambling houses, and the like, and may inquire as to the condition of the poor in their district. When a petition for a local improvement is presented to the president of a borough board, he must call a meeting of the local board within fifteen days, and if that board recommends that the work be done, a resolution to that effect must be adopted, and a copy sent to the department of public improvements.

On January 1, 1898, the new city came into existence, with Robert A. Van Wyck, who had been elected as the candidate of the Democratic party the November previous, as its first mayor.

Before closing it will be interesting to present some statistics of Greater New York in comparison with London, Paris, and Berlin.

In population she is the second city in the world, London having 4,463,169 souls,[1] Paris 2,511,629, Berlin 1,726,098, New York 3,389,753.

In area she is the first city in the world, London having 74,672 acres, Paris 19,279, Berlin 15,662, and New York 193,850.

In public parks also she leads the cities of the earth, New York having 6,587.52 acres, London 5,976, Paris 4,739, and Berlin 1,637.

She has 1,002.34 miles of paved streets, London 1,818, Paris 604, and Berlin 500.

She has 1,156.21 miles of sewers to London's, 2,500, Paris's 599, Berlin's 465.

She has 531.84 miles of street railroad, London none, Paris 24, Berlin 225.

The assessed value of her real estate is $2,377,277,820; London's, $5,335,140,654.

Her net bonded debt is $185,081,850, that of London $200,000,000, of Paris $520,677,830, of Berlin $69,937,098.

Her annual expenses are $60,000,000, London's $65,000,000, Paris's $72,701,700, Berlin's $21,294,333.

Her daily water supply is 330,000,000 gallons, that of London 203,000,000, of Paris 136,000,000, of Berlin 30,000,000.

---

[1] Including the whole metropolitan district London has 6,291,677.

## XXVI. BROOKLYN.

FREQUENT references have been made to Brooklyn in the preceding narrative, the settlement and growth of which went on side by side with that of New York. One of the first acts of the West India Company was to buy of the Indians the whole western end of Long Island. As early as 1645 we know there were farms along the road from Flatbush to the ferry.

Brooklyn City Hall.

By 1646 nearly the whole water front had been cleared and put under cultivation, and there were small villages at the Wallabout, the ferry, and Gowanus.

The same year Kieft ordered an election for two schepens, or aldermen, for "Breuckelen," and a little later a schout, or constable. The Heights early became a favorite site for the residences of the gentry, Philip Livingston possessing a fine mansion on the east side of Hicks Street, near Joralemon, prior to 1764.

Brooklyn was incorporated as a village in 1816 (April 12), in which year the first public schoolhouse was built. It was not until 1834 that it was incorporated as a city, and then against the strenuous opposition of the assemblymen from New York, who urged that the interests of the two towns were the same, and that Brooklyn ought to be one with New York. At this time (1834) the country road, the "King's Highway" of colonial times, ran crookedly up the hill from the

Memorial Arch, Brooklyn.

"ferry slip" (now Fulton Ferry), past an old Dutch church set in the middle of the road, and on through Bedford and Jamaica to Montauk Point. The town was then well built up as far as the junction of the present Main and Fulton streets.

Meantime to the north another city was growing. Bushwick, later Williamsburgh, and later still the Eastern District of Brooklyn, was settled in 1641-1650 by a few Norman immigrants, who in March, 1660, erected a village, defended by a blockhouse, on a point of land near the foot of the present South Fifth Street, the blockhouse being intended for defense against Indians. A month before, fourteen French immigrants, with a Dutchman to teach them the arts of pioneer life, had settled near the present site of Maspeth. Bushwick was patented in 1687, with a population of seven hundred and fifty-nine souls; Williamsburgh was incorporated in April, 1827; and that city and Bushwick were annexed to Brooklyn in April, 1854, as the Eastern District.

## XXVII. THE BRONX.

IN two respects New York is now the greatest city in the world—in area, and in the variety, beauty, and magnitude of her public parks. While Central Park and Prospect Park are the pride of the city, it is not until one passes over the Harlem and wanders through the miles of forests and meadows of Van Cortlandt Park, or in Bronx Park follows the clear and silvery waters of the Bronx to the wide green levels of Pelham Bay Park, with its cool breezes and wide views of the Sound, that one appreciates the greatness of our park system, and the farsightedness of those city officials who, about 1870, began the movement that resulted in the acquiring of these forest-clad districts, to be held forever for the delight and well being of the people of the city.

Van Cortlandt Park, which lies nearest the Hudson and extends from the Yonkers line almost to Spuyten Duyvil, is two miles long by one mile wide, and contains 1,132 acres. Pelham Bay Park exceeds it, however, having 1,756 acres, while Bronx Park falls in behind with 662 acres. When you consider that Central Park contains but 840 acres, and Prospect 516⅙, you get a better idea of the magnitude of these later parks. Van Cortlandt Park comprises part of the famous old

The Bronx.

manor of Phillipseborough. The city has done little more to improve it than to lay out good roads through its forests and valleys.

If, on leaving Kingsbridge, we follow the bicyclers along the old Albany Post Road north, we shall see, shortly before reaching the Yonkers city line, the old Van Cortlandt manor house, a fine old mansion standing in the fields on our left, with wide lawns in front. It occupies the site of a blockhouse erected by Governor Dongan as an outpost and place of refuge from the Indians for hunting and scouting parties. Jacobus Van Cortlandt married Eva Phillipse, daughter of Frederick, the famous lord of Phillipseborough, and his son Frederick built the present mansion in 1748, as you may see by a stone on the southeast corner. It is now the property of the city, being included in the park, and we may enter freely. Here are the wide halls, the huge fireplaces, flanked by blue tiles bearing pictures

Van Cortlandt Manor House.

of scriptural scenes, the deep window seats where the young people found quiet retreats and their elders smoked and gravely talked in colonial days.

In the Revolution, when this section was a dark and bloody ground, and the outposts of the British and patriot armies confronted each other from these hilltops, the old house was the headquarters of the commander of the German yagers. A few days before the British left New York forever, on Evacuation Day, 1783, General Washington and his staff took up their abode here, the general making it his headquarters until he, with his army, occupied the city. The bed in which he slept is still preserved in the old house.

Because of its historical interest, the Colonial Dames of the State of New York secured a lease of it for twenty-five years, and opened there a very interesting collection of relics of the Revolution and of colonial times.

On a part of the estate is still shown an old oak on which thirty "cowboys" were hanged during the Revolution. At that time this region quite over to the Bronx, and to the Sound for that matter, lay "between the lines," and was ranged over and harried by Tories and patriots alternately, the one side being termed "cowboys," and the other "skinners." First the Tories would make a raid, and then the patriots would attack them in reprisal, while both parties plundered the peaceful Quakers without mercy.[1] By 1779 these people had become mere marauding bands, plundering both Whig and Tory impartially, and in January of that year Colonel Aaron Burr was ordered to take command of the "lines," punish the marauders, and give peace to the country. He was admirably fitted for the task, and did what others had not been able to do. First he drew a map of the country, showing all the roads and paths by which the culprits could escape. Then he made a list of all the inhabitants, putting each in his proper class, as whig, tory, half tory, spy, marauder, etc., and when an outrage was committed made every

[1] In Cooper's fine novel of "The Spy" you will find spirited accounts of the conflicts between cowboys and skinners, with graphic descriptions of the country.

suspected party give an account of himself. Then, with his men, he scouted so unceasingly, watched so vigilantly, and punished so sternly that the bands were soon broken up, and life and property became as secure as in New York or in the Continental camp.

There are several smooth, hard roads leading eastward into the beautiful valley of the Bronx. From its entrance into the Sound at Hunts Point, back through Westchester, Bronx Park, Woodlawn, Mount Vernon, Bronxville, Tuckahoe, and White Plains (where the battle was fought), to its source in the hills this side of the Croton divide, it presents every variety of sylvan and pastoral scenery, in such striking contrast with the works and homes of men as to be a source of constant surprise and delight.

# INDEX.

Adams, John, arrives in New York, 195; receives Washington, 197.
Allerton, Isaac, 58.
American Fur Company, 233.
Andros, Sir Edmund, 75; appointed governor, 78; received, 81.
Anne Queen, accession of, 103.
Antill, John, 143.
Apthorpe house, 179, 180.
*Archangel*, 90.
Arnold, Isaac, 95.
Assembly, first Provincial, 79.
Astor, John Jacob, 230.
Auchmuty, Rev. Dr. Samuel, 143.

Baltimore and Ohio Railroad, 229.
Baptists, 42.
Barlow, Joel, 216.
Barrett, Walter, quoted, 238.
Bath Beach, 153.
Battery, the, in 1830, 265.
Battle Hill in Greenwood, 168.
Bayard, Judith, 51.
Bayard, Nicholas, 47, 83, 87, 113; imprisoned, 90; released, 94.
Bayard, Samuel, 143.
Bayard, Colonel William, 143.
Bear hunt, a, 110.
*Beaver*, the, 91.
Bedford, 156, 157.
Bell, farmers', 67.
Bellomont, Earl of, 76, 113; appointed governor, 101.
*Betsy*, pioneer trading ship, 236.
Binckes, Admiral, 77.
Black Ball line, 241.
Block, Adriaen, discovers Long Island Sound, 11.
Bogardus, Domine, death of, 38.
Borough of the Bronx, 290.
Boston Post Road, described, 176.
Bowling Green, 62, 67.
Box, Fort, 155.
Bradford, Governor, claims Dutch soil, 19.
Bradford, William, printer, 104.

Bridge Street and bridge, 60.
Broad Street, 60; in 1700, 121.
Broadway, laid out, 73; in 1700, 112.
Bronx Park, 290.
Brooklyn, history of, 287.
Brooklyn church, 156.
Brooklyn Heights, 153.
Buchanan, Thomas, 144.
Burnet, William, 76.
Burr, Major Aaron, aide to Putnam, 159; rescues part of Putnam's army, 181; duel with Hamilton, 204-207; subdues cowboys and skinners, 293.

Canal Street in 1820, 261.
Capitol, first, 197.
Carleton, General, 160.
Carpesey, Gabriel, town herdsman, 66.
Castle Garden, 266.
Central Park, 271.
Chambers, Captain, 148-150.
Charles, King, death of, 80.
Charter, Great, 81, 82.
Charter of Liberties and Privileges, 80.
Charter of New Amsterdam, 38; city proclaimed, 39.
China trade, 232.
Churchgoing in New Amsterdam, 68.
Church service, 70, 71.
City Hall, new, 121; used as an arsenal, 151; built, 263.
City Hall Park, 66; in 1830, 263.
City wall (second), 117.
Civil War, outbreak of, 250-254.
*Clermont*, 215.
Clinton, De Witt, 221, 226.
Clinton, George, 76, 193.
Clipper ships, 242.
Coast Road, 157.
Coffeehouses, 131.
Colden, Lieutenant Governor, 139, 143.
Collect, the, 118.
Columbia College, founded, 197.
Colyer, Vincent, 255.

Committee of Correspondence, appointed, 139.
Common, public meetings on, 146.
Coney Island, 153.
Congress, first sits in New York, 195; removes to Philadelphia, 202.
Continental uniforms, 157.
Cooper, Rev. Dr. Myles, 143.
Cooper's, Peter, store, 262.
Cornbury, Lord, 76.
Cortelyou, Jacques, 112.
Cortelyou house, 170.
Cosby, Alexander, 123.
Cosby, William, governor, 76, 120; orders trial of Zenger, 105.
Craft, colonial, 56, 57.
Cregier, Marten, 63.
Croton water, introduced, 268.
Cruger, John H., 143.
Cunard, Samuel, founds Cunard line, 249.
Cuyler, Lieutenant, 85.

Damen, Jan Jansen, 74.
De Hart, Simon, 112.
De Lancey, Chief Justice, James, tries Zenger, 105, 113.
Delaware, Lackawanna and Western Railroad, 229.
Dellius, Domine, land grant to, 102.
De Peyster, Captain, 85.
De Riemer, Isaac, 113, 122.
Dircksen, Cornelis, 72.
Dix, Dorothea L., 255.
Dix, John A., 254.
Docks, city, 55, 124.
*Dolphin*, the, 7.
Dongan, Thomas, 75, 85; appointed governor, 79.
Dress in 1700, 112.
Duane, James, 193.
Dudley, Chief Justice, presides at trial of Leisler, 95.
Duke's Farm, 74.
Duke's Laws, 76.
Dunmore, Earl of, 76.
Dunscomb, 165.
Dutch, capture New York, 77.
Dutch, description of, 9, 10.
Dutch bed, 67.
Dutch church, 112.
Dutch dress, 69.
Dutch manners and customs, 52–57.

East India Company, Dutch, the, 10.
East New York, 156.
East River Bridge, 275.
Eastern Boulevard, the, 153.
Eelkens, Jacob, arrives in trading ship *William*, 24; ordered away, 25; removed by the Dutch, 27.

English, capture Manhattan, 49; discover New York Bay, 10; claim Manhattan, 19.
Erie Canal, account of, 220; celebration at opening of, 222, 223.
Erie Railroad, opened, 228.
Evergreen Cemetery, 165.
Evertsen, Admiral, 77.

Ferry ordinances, 72.
Ferryboats, 134.
Fire company, 118.
Fire department, 133.
Fire engines, 133.
Fish, 67.
Fish, Nicholas, 159.
Fitz Roy, Lord Augustus, 122.
Flatbush, 156.
Flatlands, 153.
Fletcher, Benjamin, 76; appointed governor, 99; founds Trinity Church, 100; scandal against, 100; recalled, 101; demands a trial, 102.
Fort, the, 62.
Fortifications of New York, 174.
Fraunces's Tavern, 149.
Fredericke, Kryn, 18.
Freedom of the city, conferred, 123.
Freeman, Thomas, 123.
Fulton, Robert, sketch of, 215.
Fulton Ferry, 52, 71.
Fur trade, Canada, 231.

Gage, Thomas, General, 143.
Game, 66.
Gas, introduced into New York, 267.
"Gazette," first newspaper in New York, 103.
George, Fort, 119; garrison of, 119.
George III., statue of, 260.
Gilliland, 165.
Governors of New York colony, 75.
Gowanus Canal, 153, and Creek, 155.
Graft officer, 60.
Grange, the, 208.
Gravesend, 156.
Gravesend Bay, 153, 162.
Greene, Fort, 156.
Greene, General, 158.
Greenwood Cemetery, 153, 156.
Griffiths, John, 143.
Griswold, N. L. & G., 237.

Hale, Nathan, executed, 187.
*Half Moon*, enters New York Bay, 9.
Halfway House, William Howard's, 165.
Hamilton, Alexander, 159, 204; death of, 209; sketch of, 210, 211.
Hamilton, Andrew, defends Zenger, 106.

Hamilton, Fort, 153, 162.
Hardy, Sir Charles, 76; lays corner stone of Columbia College, 108.
Harlem Heights, 174, 175; described, 181; battle of, 182–184.
Heath, General, 158.
Heights of Guana, 156, 157.
Hendrik, Fort William, 78.
"Herald," founded, 264.
Hessians, arrive, 160.
Hicks, Jasper, 95.
Hoogland, 165.
Horsmanden, Daniel, 143.
Howe, Sir William, invests New York, 152; offers amnesty, 160.
Howland & Aspinwall, 236.
Hudson, Henry, discovers New York Bay, 10.
Hudson Bay Fur Company, 231.
Hunter, Robert, 76.

Indians, sell Manhattan Island, 15; trade with Dutch, 18; attack Dutch, 30; submit, 32; attack Manhattan, 41; hunting party of, 66.
Ingoldsby, Richard, lieutenant governor, 90; arrives, 91, 92; demands surrender of fort, 93, 94; tries Leisler, 95.
Irving, Washington, 235.

Jamaica, 156, 157.
Jamaica Pass, unguarded, 164.
James, Fort, 77.
James, King, 80.
Jans, Annetje, farm, 74; given to Trinity Church, 103.
Johnson, Samuel, president Columbia College, 107.
Johnson, Thomas, 95.
"Journal, Holt's," quoted, 147.
Jumel mansion, 182.

Kidd, Captain, account of, 126.
Kieft, Wilhelm, chosen director, 28; arrival, 29; becomes dictator, 30; at war with Indians, 31, 32; calls a council, 31; recalled, 34; prosecutes his accusers, 37; death, 38.
King's Farm, 74; given to Trinity Church, 103.
King's Highway, 156.
Kip, Abraham, 117.
Knowlton, Colonel Thomas, 182.
Knox, General, 158.
Kuyter, Joachim Pietersen, 37, 38.

Labadists, the, quoted, 111.
Lafayette, arrival in New York, 266.
Lamb, John, 144, 151.
Lehigh Valley Railroad, 229.

Leisler, Jacob, 84; seizes government, 86; trial of, 95; death of, 97; estate restored, 98, 101.
Leitch, Major, 183.
L'Enfant, Pierre, remodels capitol, 197.
Le Roux, Charles, 123.
Liberty pole, erected, 145; causes a riot, 146.
Lind, Jenny, 266.
Livingston, Phillip and Robert, 162.
Livingston, Robert, 127, 217.
Lockyer, Captain, 147.
*London*, tea ship, 148.
Long Island, battle of, 159–170; British troops in, 159; British commanders in, 159; American position, 163; British position, 162, 163; British advance, 164; British attack American rear, 166; retreat from, 172.
Long Island City, 280.
Loockermans, Govert, 58.
Lovelace, Francis, 76; governor, 77.
Lutherans, 42.

Mackinaw Fur Company, 231.
Magaw, Colonel Robert, 184.
Maiden Lane, 53.
Manhattan Island, described, 14; purchased, 15; first settled, 13.
Manning, Captain, 77.
Markets of New York, 129.
Martense Lane, 157.
Massacre, Boston, 147.
McComb mansion, 202.
McDougall, Alexander, 144.
Megapolensis, Domine, 48.
Melyn, Cornelis, 37, 38.
Merchants' Exchange, first, 61.
Merchants, great, of New York, 58, 238.
Merrymaking in New York, 119.
Michaelis, Rev. Jonas, arrives, 18.
Millborne, Jacob, 84; trial of, 95; death of, 97; estate restored, 101.
Minuit, Peter, first governor of New Netherlands, arrives, 14; purchases island, 15; his powers, 16, and government, 17; communicates with Governor Bradford, 19; recalled, 22.
Minvielle, Gabriel, 113.
Mohawk and Hudson Railroad, 228.
Mohawk Indians, declare against Leisler, 97.
Mohawks of New York, 147, 149.
Monckton, Robert, 76.
Montague's Tavern, 146.
Montgomery, Lord John, 76.
Moore, Sir Henry, 76, 144; orders soldiers to keep the peace, 146; mentioned, 147.

Morningside Park, 271.
Murray's Wharf, 150.

Nancy, first tea ship, 147, 148.
Navy Yard, 153.
Negro plot, 116.
New Amsterdam, settled, 14; captured by the English, 43; manners and customs in, 52; population of, in 1664, 74.
New Orange, 78.
Newspaper extracts, 116.
New Utrecht, 112, 156.
New Year's observances, 110.
New York, taken by the English and named, 43-49; attacked by Dutch, 77; bounds of, 79; joined to New England, 81; under British rule, 109; attacked by British, 179; retreat from, 181; captured by British, 179, 181; in 1776, 176; in captivity, 186; great fire in, 186; evacuated by British, 192; first capital, 195; official life in, 1789-1790, 200; no longer the capital, 202; commercial growth, 214; in Civil War, 254; in 1783, 272; in 1830, 272; in 1850, 273; in 1865, 274; in 1870, 276; part of Westchester County annexed, 277; consolidation of, 279; charter of, 280; compared with London, Paris, and Berlin, 286.
New York Central and Hudson River Railroad, 229.
New York Historical Society, sketch of, 212.
Nicholson, Lieutenant Governor, 83; sails for England, 86; appointed lieutenant governor of Virginia, 89.
Nicolls, Colonel Richard, captures Manhattan, 43-49; mentioned, 75.
Nicolls, William, 90; released, 94.
Noell, Thomas, assumes mayoralty, 122.
Northwest Fur Company, 231.

Ocean Parkway, 153.
Orange, Fort, 26.
Ordinances, Dutch, 64.
Osborne, Sir Danvers, 76.
Osgood mansion, 202.

Packet ships, 240.
Park Theater, 263.
Parties in New York, 143; after the Revolution, 203.
Patroons, established, 20.
Pauw, Michael de, 22; purchases Staten Island, 22.
Pear tree, Stuyvesant's, 50.
Pearl Street, 52.

Pelham Bay Park, 290.
Pennsylvania Railroad, 229.
Phillipse, Adolph, 128.
Phillipse, Frederick, 83; justice, 105.
Phillipse manor house, 83.
Pinhorn, recorder, 95.
Pirates and privateersmen, 100, 101, 124; names of their vessels, 125.
Plays in New York, 134.
Ploughman, collector, 85.
Prison ships, 188.
Prisons, military, in New York, 188.
Prospect Park, 153, 156.
Public parks, 270, 290.
Putnam, Fort, 156.
Putnam, Israel, in New York, 152, 158; succeeds Sullivan, 163.

Quackenbos, Walter, 146.
Quakers, the, 42.

Rapalje, Sarah, 19.
Rasières, Isaac de, 20.
Red Lion Tavern, 157, 164.
Rensselaerwyck, founded, 21.
Revolution, first blood of, spilled in New York, 147.
Riot, Draft, in New York, 256-258.
Riverside Park, 271.
Robinson, John, 110.
Robinson, Sir Robert, 95.
Rogers, Captain Moses, 246.

Saint Mark's Church, founded, 51.
Scott, John Morin, 144.
Sea Mew, the, 14.
Seal of New Amsterdam, 40.
Sears, Isaac, 144, 146, 151.
Servants, 116.
Shoemakers Creek, 165.
Slaves, negro, 116.
Sloughter, Henry, 75; appointed governor, 89; arrives in New York, 93; death, 99.
Smit, Claes, 31.
Smith, Colonel William, 95; defends Zenger, 105.
Smith, William, historian, quoted, 109.
Sons of Liberty, 144, 146, 147; in control of New York, 152.
Spencer, General, 158.
Staats, Dr. Samuel, 113.
Stadt Huys, built by Kieft, 34, 55.
Stages, Broadway, 259.
Stamp Act, 136.
Stamp Act riot, the, 140.
Steamboats, 215; invented, 217.
Steamers, the first, 246.
Steenwyck, Cornelis, 46, 58.
Stirling, Fort, 155.
Street car lines, 268.

Street venders, 1830, 265.
Stoll, Sergeant, 86.
Stores and merchants of New York, 1705, 128.
Stuyvesant, Petrus, chosen director, 34; character, 35; arrival, 35, 36; gives charter, 38, and seal, 40; attacks the Swedes, 41; placates the Indians, 42; yields to the English, 49; death, 49; mentioned, 70.
Sugarhouse, 188.
Sullivan, General, 158; his troops engaged, 167.
"Sun," founded, 264.
"Swamp," the, 118.

Tammany Hall, 264.
Tammany Society, sketch of, 212.
Tea ships, the, 138.
Tea Party, Boston's, 147.
Tea Party, New York's, 147.
Theaters, 134.
"Times," founded, 264.
"Tribune," founded, 264.
Trinity Church, endowed, 74; opened, 112; account of, 123.
Tryon, Sir William, 76; character of, 147; in England, 151; returns to New York, 152.
Tupper, Benjamin, commands whaleboat fleet, 159, 160.
Tweed Ring, 276.

Union Defense Committee, organized, 254.

Van Cortlandt, Stephanus, mayor, 83, 87, 88.
Van Cortlandt Park, 290.
Van Cortlandt manor house, 291.
Vanderbilt, Cornelius, 217, 218.
Van der Grist, schepen, wounded by Indians, 41.
Vanderveer, Pieter Cornelissen, 58.
Van Dinclage, 36, 37.
Van Dyck, Hendrik, 32.
Van Dyck, ex-sheriff, killed by Indians, 41.
Van Rensselaer, Kiliaen, 21.

Van Twiller, Wouter, chosen director, 23; described, 23; his arrival, 24; attacks the English, 27, 28; removed, 28.
Van Wagener, 165.
Vauxhall Gardens, 262.
Verrazano, Jean, discovers Bay of New York, 7.
Vlie boats, 63.
Vries, De, patroon, 24; purchases Staten Island, 28; his plantation ravaged by Indians, 30, 42.

Walk down Broadway, 259.
Wall, city, 53.
Wall Street, 53.
Wallabout Bay, 155.
Walloon yeomen, 71.
Walloons, settle New Netherlands, 13.
Washington, passes through New York, 152; takes command on Long Island, 169; retreats from Long Island, 172; takes leave of his officers, 193; inaugurated, 196; his levees, 202.
Washington, Fort, 184.
Washington Park, 153.
West India Company, described, 12.
West Shore Railroad, 229.
Whaleboat fleet, 159.
Whitehall Street, 61.
Whitehall mansion, 61.
Willett, Marinus, 144.
William of Orange, king, 81; approves Leisler's sentence, 98; death of, 103.
William Henry, Fort, 122.
Williamsburgh, 289.
Winthrop, Governor, 46, 77.
Wolves, bounty on, 64.
Woman's Central Relief Association, 255.
Wooley, Rev. James, quoted, 110.
"World," founded 264.

Young, John, 95.

Zenger, John Peter, founds "Weekly Journal," 104; trial of, for libel, 105; acquitted, 107.

www.ingramcontent.com/pod-product-compliance
Lightning Source LLC
Chambersburg PA
CBHW022112230426
43672CB00008B/1354